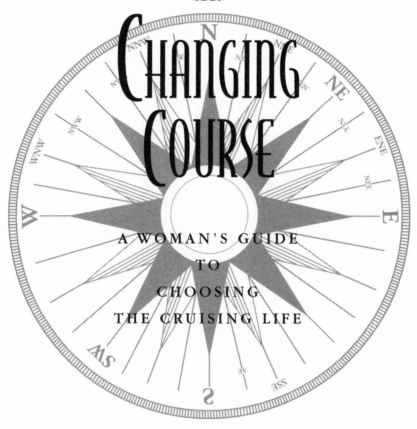

# CHANGING COURSE

## A WOMAN'S GUIDE
## TO
## CHOOSING
## THE CRUISING LIFE

# DEBRA ANN CANTRELL

INTERNATIONAL MARINE / McGRAW-HILL
Camden, Maine • New York • San Francisco • Washington, D.C.
Auckland • Bogotá • Caracas • Lisbon • London • Madrid • Mexico City
Milan • Montreal • New Delhi • San Juan • Singapore • Sydney • Tokyo • Toronto

〜‎ ‎〜

*For Jim, my partner in change, and the love of my life*

**International Marine**   ℛ
A Division of The *McGraw-Hill* Companies

10 9 8 7 6 5 4 3 2 1

*Library of Congress Cataloging-in-Publication Data*
Cantrell, Debra Ann, 1957–
    Changing Course : a woman's guide to choosing the cruising life / Debra Ann Cantrell.
        p.    cm.
    Includes bibliographical references.
    ISBN 0-07-136087-5 (alk. paper)
    1. Boating for women. 2. Boat living. I. Title.
GV777.57.C25 2000
797.1'082—dc21                                                    00-033600

Questions regarding the content of this book should be addressed to
International Marine
P.O. Box 220
Camden, ME 04843
http://www.internationalmarine.com

Questions regarding the ordering of this book should be addressed to
The McGraw-Hill Companies
Customer Service Department
P.O. Box 547
Blacklick, OH 43004
Retail customers: 1-800-262-4729
Bookstores: 1-800-722-4726

This book is printed on 55# Sebago.
Printed by R.R. Donnelley, Crawfordsville, IN
Design by Dede Cummings Design
Production Management by Janet Robbins
Edited by Jon Eaton and Cynthia Flanagan Goss

# Contents

# Acknowledgments

A BOOK IS NEVER THE CREATION OF ONE individual, and this book is no exception.

I am especially grateful to the women who faxed, wrote, and in some instances phoned from around the world to share their stories. Their interest, enthusiasm, investment in time, and constant urgings to write this book—both for them, and for those who are contemplating walking where they have tread—was a constant source of inspiration. May I one day be as wise, courageous, and skilled as every one of them.

At least half the excitement of this undertaking has come from sharing my progress with interested family and friends, and the cruisers and would-be cruisers I have met along the way. In particular, I am thankful to my wonderful friend and mother-in-law Lucie, who has been an enduring source of support, encouragement, and inspiration from start to finish; to my special friends Allen and Gretchen, who assuaged many of my fears, encouraged my respect for the sea, and are living proof that cruising friends share lifelong bonds; and to my good friends Peter and Nancy, whose interest in my tales, tribulations, and triumphs never wavered. Their embracing of the cruising life at a time when their same-age peers were taking more predictable routes is especially inspiring.

I am blessed with close family and friends who were supportive and understanding and never complained or abandoned ship when I was immersed in writing for weeks on end.

Jon Eaton and Deborah Oliver of International Marine deserve special mention for believing in my book and offering advice and helpful suggestions throughout the duration of this project.

I reserve deepest gratitude for my partner, Jim, for his unconditional and unwavering support. He has continuously nurtured me and my ideas and has always believed in me—even when I didn't believe in myself. His technical wizardry also made it possible for me to write parts of this book on the aft deck of *Red Witch* in the north and *Beedahbun* in the south. It was on these vessels, with laptop in hand, that I was continuously inspired by the very same elements that inspired many women to move their lives to the water: gentle breezes, rippling water, and freedom from the day-to-day clutter that so often distracts us from what matters most in life.

A NOTE ABOUT EPIGRAPHS

Over the past twenty-five years I have collected and filed quotations from a vast variety of sources—books, magazines, public speeches, newspaper articles, greeting cards, etc.—that I have found to be especially inspiring, encouraging, or thought provoking.

As *Changing Course* evolved, it seemed appropriate that quotes from my collection should open each chapter. But the quotes, not having been saved for publication and coming as they do from such disparate sources, are not always attributed beyond the individual quoted. Sorting through this dilemma has been instructive. When a quotation was attributed to an individual, I noted this with care. I have included sources of quotations in the bibliography.

I gratefully acknowledge the individuals to whom quotations are attributed and thank them for their inspiring and encouraging words of wisdom.

We cannot reach new horizons
if we fear to leave the shore.

# Introduction

IMAGINE FOR A MOMENT THAT YOU HAVE A job you love, a partner who adores you, a home that's an inspiring space for work and play, and enough combined income to indulge in whatever interests strike your fancy: you have reached a place in your life that you never imagined possible, and you feel blessed. Then one day, your partner casually says, "What do you think of the idea of living on a boat someday, of having the freedom and the time to travel around the world, learn about other cultures, learn another language or two?"

You might jump up and down and exclaim, "When do we leave?" You might count to ten, take a deep breath, and hope this is only a passing fantasy. You might, as I did, feel immediately anxious as you try to reconcile the implications of two very different lifestyles—one lived on land, and one lived on water.

My partner's desire to live on a boat and go cruising was the impetus to a five-year study I conducted to explore how others coped with their partner's desire to make a similar lifestyle change. That study is the foundation of this book.

The study's participants were women, for I learned that the majority of couples who embark upon the cruising lifestyle often do so at the strenuous insistence of the male partner and the equally strenuous resistance of their female mates. There are exceptions, however; some women embraced the cruising life from the outset; a few were even initiators.

I found these women through a letter posted in *Cruising World* magazine and in a national Canadian newspaper, and via word of mouth. Respondents completed an initial questionnaire and were later interviewed. A group of 107 women at various stages of entering the cruising life participated (see the appendix for demographic information about the study's participants and for sample questions).

In candid and often poignant detail, these women described the various aspects of the cruising lifestyle that profoundly affected their lives. Each woman's story is unique, but they share similar thoughts, feelings, and behaviors—from their reactions to their partner's proposed change, to the steps they took to make the cruising lifestyle a reality. In just about every instance, this change in lifestyle evolved from one that was externally imposed (by him) and initially resisted (by her), to one that was embraced by both partners.

*Changing Course* is the first book of its kind to focus on the cruising lifestyle as experienced by the *partner* of the person who initiated the move to this new life. It is more than a book about how to successfully move from land to sea. It is about the odyssey of change: our fear of casting off the familiar for an unknown shore and what we stand to gain when we do. This book may help you change your life by offering practical strategies that will inspire you to look beyond your current lifestyle and see the rewards in a new way of life.

Learning about the experiences of other women helped me to make a change and thrive in a new lifestyle. My journey was reinforced by the discovery that I was not alone.

I hope you too will be inspired by the thoughts, feelings, and experiences of the remarkable women in this book who set sail with ambivalence and a little trepidation, only to rediscover themselves and their relationships and to reshape their lives into ones that became more rewarding and meaningful.

# Going Cruising: An Odyssey of Change

"Life is either a daring adventure or nothing."

HELEN KELLER

I HAVE NEVER FORGOTTEN THE BLUSTERY day my husband Jim casually mentioned that he thought it would be fun to live on a boat someday. That day is especially memorable because it was the tenth anniversary of the sinking of the *Edmund Fitzgerald* on Lake Superior. Throughout the day, the local radio stations played Gordon Lightfoot's tribute to the ship and her crew, all of whom were lost when the vessel was battered by hurricane-force winds and gargantuan waves. As I listened to Lightfoot croon about the mishap I thanked God I was safe on land, basking in the warmth of a fireplace while winds howled outside and torrential rains fell throughout the night.

I was afraid of the water. Terrified, actually. Throughout my early adult years, I was plagued by the same recurring dream of being swept below the surface of a frothing black sea by a monstrous wave and drowning. I cannot attribute my fear to a specific event; it is more likely a combination of childhood experiences that became distorted over time.

I grew up fearing the water, not only because I was afraid of drowning but also because I feared the creatures I imagined lurking below the surface. I could not spend time in the water without constantly pirouetting about, carefully surveying the surface for the shape of a fin. I equated living on a boat with man-eating sharks and rogue waves—and I was at a loss to understand how such a dangerous environment would be attractive to anyone.

As my partner talked about how liberating it would be to live on a boat and explore the world, I recall thinking, "What could possibly be so liberating about living in a small space in such a perilous environment?" As he espoused the virtues of the cruising life—of a more simplistic, less materialistic, less encumbered lifestyle on a boat—all I could imagine was the black hole I risked falling into if this sudden dream of his became a reality.

With his idea hardly a breath in the making, I immediately began to mourn my perceived losses: a career I loved; a home and yard that had become my psychological sanctuary; a wine cellar that I'd taken such care to assemble over the past ten years; my prized lily garden. But more than anything, it was my career that I feared losing because it had long defined who I was and fed my self-esteem. I had spent fifteen years developing a lucrative private practice as a training and capacity-building specialist with a primarily aboriginal client population. My practice had evolved and expanded: in addition to hands-on training, I was integrating my own philosophy of holistic wellness with what I had learned from aboriginal elders and sharing this with others who were interested in bringing more balance to their lives. I considered the idea of living on a boat to be a major interruption in my career rather than a means of enhancing my life.

I needed to consider a change in lifestyle carefully before I embarked upon my partner's dream, so I set out to learn about the women who went before me. What became of the ambivalent partners, the women who sailed away from home, community, a family, and/or a career to follow their partner's dream of living on a boat and sailing around the world? My five-year study of over a hundred women who faced a similar situation gave me the answers I needed.

When my husband first introduced the idea of moving onto a boat, it was difficult for me to imagine that such a change in lifestyle could reveal untold benefits and opportunities for personal growth and revitalization. But that is exactly what happened. That move to a different kind of lifestyle became a journey of exploration and discovery that forever changed my life, and it was the same for many of the women whose stories are in this book. For many, moving on board a boat became a defining phase in their lives: their own odyssey of change.

## GOING CRUISING: PART OF A LARGER TREND

Cashing Out. The Spirit Moves Them. Leaving Fast Track Behind. The Simple Life. Headlines such as these began to dominate the news in the early 1990s. If these headlines represent a trend, and experts say they do, then increasing numbers of North Americans are endeavoring to live their dreams by making significant lifestyle changes. Most are seeking a simpler, slower-paced lifestyle that is characterized by inner peace and fulfillment versus excessive consumerism. Moving to a life on the water and going cruising is part of this prevalent trend.

Some look for a simpler life in the countryside, such as the female executive who surprised her Wall Street colleagues by quitting to become a sheep farmer; she traded the confines of the office and the boardroom for pastures and rolling hills. Some opt for an open-air studio where they aspire to sell their art for a living (or failing that, have great fun imagining themselves to be the next van Gogh or Hemingway). Those who are eager for an even less encumbered lifestyle go cruising.

An increasing number of people are realizing the dream of sailing off into the sunset. Containing your earthly goods in a small floating space and exploring the world on that floating home is to some the picture of ultimate freedom. Cruising is a life characterized by the beauty and tranquility of the water, communion with nature, freedom from the encumbrances of a traditional land-based lifestyle, and the romance of travel. For many, the cruising life represents simplicity and self-sufficiency in their purest forms.

**For many cruisers, the cruising life represents simplicity and self-sufficiency in their purest forms.**

The desire to live aboard a boat and cruise the waterways of the world is not confined to any particular age group or income bracket. Individuals and couples in their early 20s and retirees well into their 60s and 70s are pursuing the cruising life with equal vigor, and cruising families of six and more are not uncommon. Living on a boat is not a lifestyle being pursued only by the rich. Cruisers cross economic boundaries, and more people are proving that the cruising lifestyle can be enjoyed on just about any budget.

Moreover, the notion that sailing around the world requires many years of experience and special talents and skills is also being dispelled. Technological advances enable those who possess good common sense, and the time and intelligence to learn how to properly operate their boat and its equipment, to set sail.

There is no doubt that the cruising lifestyle requires greater self-sufficiency than life on land. For example, many of the conveniences we generally take for granted on land are harder to come by on the water, including unlimited electricity, fresh water, garbage pickup, and unrestricted sewage disposal. But that push toward being more self-sufficient has its rewards.

The trend toward simpler lifestyles, where many individuals are choosing to live with less, constitutes more than a reduction in spending habits: it represents a fundamental shift in values, and many people suddenly discover they have a greater purpose in life than material gain. Most of these people pursued the American dream, worked hard, raised their children, and were rewarded with money to buy more "stuff"—only to discover that their material successes did not make them feel content or fulfilled.

The cruising life provides an ideal opportunity to shift from a lifestyle dominated by material gain to one in which simplicity, self-reliance, and personal and spiritual discovery take precedence.

## THE PROSPECT OF A NEW LIFE: A DEFINING MOMENT

As ideal as cruising sounds, moving aboard a boat and sailing around the world may not be the life you would choose—but it may be a life that has become your partner's dream. Hearing about her partner's desire to live on a boat was a defining moment for almost every woman I interviewed. For Terry, age 39, that moment "changed everything. I wanted the whole idea to just go away. But knowing that he wanted to live on a boat and that I did not was something that I thought about all the time."

For others, their partner's dream nearly became a tangible object that pervaded their thoughts and their relationship. Going cruising "was like a large black cloud that hung over us, affecting everything we talked about—even when we didn't talk about [it]."

But feelings evolve. Over time, many women's initial shock, anger, and resistance merged with a sense of curiosity, excitement, and intrigue. Several factors affected the degree to which those feelings changed and the time it took for that shift to occur. First was the sense of loss women felt when they thought about leaving their current life.

### GRIEVING A LIFE LEFT BEHIND

When many women encountered the idea of going cruising, they felt a sense of loss over the prospect of leaving the life they knew and enjoyed behind. It is a feeling that is not unlike grieving the loss of a loved one. While their sense of losing a lifestyle is not as profound as losing someone they love, the prospect of having to leave their lives behind initially cast a shadow on their land-based lifestyles.

Some women found themselves suddenly questioning the value of their life on land; a few pondered what factors may have caused their partners to become so disillusioned with their current lives; many blamed themselves for somehow having failed to make land-based life interesting enough to retain their partner's interest.

Beyond this general sense of loss, many women in the study identified specific areas of loss as they moved further ahead in their decision to go cruising. Factors such as losing close proximity to family and having to leave careers they had worked hard to build were among their concerns.

I discuss these issues in detail in chapter 3 and share how these women compensated and, as a result, experienced personal growth. A key factor in managing these issues was having a supportive partner.

### WHAT ABOUT MY DREAMS?

The other factor that ruled how the feelings of these women evolved after their initial encounter with the idea of going cruising was the extent to which their own dreams seemed to be displaced by this lifestyle change.

I had long dreamed of bicycling across Europe and someday trading homes for extended periods with someone who lived in the south of France or northern Italy. My partner assured me that my dreams did not have to end when we went cruising. "Why can't a boat be our home as we travel through Europe?" he asked. "In fact," he continued, "we would enjoy greater access to much of Europe if we lived aboard a boat. We can do the things you want to do—maybe not exactly as you imagined them, but we can do them nevertheless."

He was right. But until I discovered that my dreams and my partner's dreams could coexist, I remained opposed to making a change that I felt was of little benefit to me personally.

For some women in the study, it was more than a case of simply looking at each person's dreams from a new angle. Merging different dreams took some planning, such as in Marilyn's case.

Marilyn wanted to go to graduate school once her children were grown and finished with college. But, "When [my partner] said he wanted to go cruising my first reaction was, 'Hey wait a minute; I've got plans, too!'" she said. "We talked about this and together came up with the idea that if I applied to a school located on the coast, we could live on the boat while I went to school. When I was done we'd sail off. I did some investigating and found out I could complete most of my course work through a distance education program. On the boat, I'd be less distracted and probably better disciplined. This is what we eventually did."

For some, it was not simply a case of forgoing their own dreams but fearing they would become the person who kept their partner from pursuing his. "I knew he had his heart set on [going cruising], and I didn't want to be the one who stood between him and his dream," said Dorothy, age 71. "I resented this feeling, though. It made me feel like I was the bad guy."

In some cases, women in this situation chose not to go cruising. They explored the idea and realized the lifestyle was not for them, so they stayed in the relationship but remained on land while their partner pursued his dream on his own.

> **"I knew he had his heart set on [going cruising], and I didn't want to be the one who stood between him and his dream."**
>
> DOROTHY

For Katherine, age 33, the issue of dreams was far less clear, for she had not taken time to define what her own dreams were. "It's not that [my dreams] are any great secret. It's just that we've focused for so long on his dream that I forgot what mine were."

If you find yourself in Katherine's situation, take some time to look at your own dreams.

---

## DEFINING YOUR OWN DREAMS

All of us have dreams. Sometimes they are at the forefront of our consciousness and other times they are buried beneath the day-to-day clutter that assumes greater immediacy in our lives. Take a moment to identify your own dreams. It's not enough to simply think about them: write them down, then ask yourself these questions.

1. Does my partner know I have these dreams? Don't assume that he does. Have you actually vocalized your dreams to him?

2. Which of my dreams can coexist with his? Which dreams can I achieve or work toward while we are cruising?

3. Which dreams am I willing to defer to a later time?

Now reexamine your list of dreams. Cross off the ones that you will have to forfeit permanently if you go cruising. There is a good chance that you did not have to strike anything from your list.

---

## HOW SOON CAN WE LEAVE?

Not all women responded with shock and resistance to their partner's idea of going cruising. Several women, while somewhat surprised by their partner's revelation, were delighted by the prospect of doing something unconventional (20 percent).

"I was thrilled when he suggested exactly what I had long wanted to do," said one woman. Others reported thinking their partner's idea sounded better than anything they could think of. For some, the idea of making a major lifestyle change came at a time when they were feeling the need for some type of change, but they had not yet envisioned what that change might be.

"I was where I wanted to be in my career, and I did not aspire to go any further in my field," said Liz, a woman in her mid-50s. "Years ago I bought the car of my dreams and now the car needed to be replaced. I thought, 'Is this all there is?' So when [he] said, 'Why don't we go cruising?' I thought, 'Why not?'"

For Meg, age 32, her partner's discussion about going cruising came with a marriage proposal, and it was the start of a new life for both of them. "John and I had lived together for seven years when he said, 'Meg, could you see yourself living on a boat with me and maybe sailing around the world one day?' I told him, 'As long as I can have a hot shower every day and you don't grow impatient with me'—I don't know how to sail—'I'd love to.' He said, 'Then marry me!'"

Meg said yes, to marriage and to the cruising life. "We've been cruising three years," she said, "It's unlike anything I've done before. Every experience is a first, and I've learned so much. We'll return to land one day, but for now we're happy seeing the world."

## TAKING A CHANCE ON A NEW LIFE

There have been many times when I have thought, "Life is good, and it can't possibly get any better." But then, when I least expect it, an opportunity arises that opens new possibilities and enhances my life in ways I never imagined.

In his book *Expand Your Life*, Dr. Allen Tough believes that "OK" lives can be enriched. "All of us find ourselves, from time to time, too comfortably habituated to a limited range of activities and interests," he says. "Sadly, most people, most of the time, pass up the majority of opportunities merely because they have never become aware of them."

Becoming aware of new possibilities is one step: taking the plunge and pursuing them is yet another matter.

A life without change is a life void of vitality, passion, and joy. But in order to change, we have to take risks. We have to deal with the conflict between our sense of comfort, contentment, and security and the frightening but exhilarating prospect of change.

Major life changes are not made easily because we essentially fear two outcomes: loss and failure. That sense of loss and failure can manifest itself in "what-if" thinking—and that type of thinking prevents many individuals from taking risks of any kind.

You may have created your own set of what-ifs as you contemplate your partner's desire to make a lifestyle change. You may wonder, "What if I find living on a boat too confining? What happens if we run into bad weather? What if I discover that I don't like being alone with my partner and that I miss the day-to-day contact with my family and friends?"

Take a few minutes and turn those questions around so they focus on a positive outcome. What if you find you love living in a small space because there is that much less space to clean? What if you run into bad weather and you are forced to stay in port and explore the area, or go cycling, or visit museums, or go shell-hunting until the weather clears? What if your relationship with your husband is renewed and you feel like you're on a second honeymoon?

Many perceive risk as something that is negative and focuses primarily on the probability of loss. For example, when someone asks, "What are the risks involved?" they are essentially asking, "What do I stand to lose?" But in fact, risk-taking is as much about the probability of gains as it is about the probability of losses.

The prospect of sailing around the world is about risk-taking: risking that you may rediscover yourself and your relationship and learn about the new people and places you encounter along the way. As the novelist Erica Jong said, "The trouble is, if you don't risk anything, you risk even more." Sometimes *not* taking a risk may cause you to lose even more.

Consider too that taking a chance on a new life may not be an opportunity that will always be available to you. For Marg, one of the women I interviewed, her father's story reminded her of this fact in poignant detail.

> **"When you're my age, you won't derive near as much comfort from reflecting on your career as you will from the memories of faraway places and people you've met along the way."**
>
> MARG'S FATHER

"When I was your age, I wanted nothing more than to sell everything lock, stock, and barrel and do something that would give me a real sense of purpose in my life," Marg's father told her.

"I'd always harbored the dream of sailing around the world someday. Your mother and I talked about maybe one day, when you kids were on your own and we'd accumulated a little nest egg, we'd buy a boat and see what would happen. But that day never came. We waited too long."

As Marg's father's arthritis worsened, he realized that he could never sail around the world. "Don't lose your chance," he told her. "Jobs are a dime a dozen. When you're my age, you won't derive near as much comfort from reflecting on your career as you will from the memories of faraway places and people you've met along the way."

## UNDERSTANDING CHANGE

By taking a step back and looking at the nature of change itself, it is easier to figure out how you can best deal with it. Here, I have classified change into three different categories.

*Self-initiated* change is internally motivated and chosen intentionally. Examples would be changing your career, quitting smoking, or downsizing to a country life. When you make a self-initiated change, you relinquish one experience and choose another, but the gains are perceived as being greater than the losses.

*Adaptive or gradual* change may be something you choose or something imposed on you. Some examples are: adjusting to living with someone after living alone for years, adapting to a new work promotion, or adjusting to life in a foreign culture.

*Radical or imposed* change is primarily caused by external forces that are thrust upon you with little warning, such as being fired, or the death of a loved one, or learning that your partner wants to make a major change in lifestyle and go cruising.

Of the three types of change, radical or imposed change is considered the most difficult to deal with. As we discussed above, it is perceived as involving a loss. It can also overwhelm you with a sense of powerlessness, leaving you to feel as if you are at the mercy of forces far stronger than you are.

But an imposed change is one you can adapt to and eventually strive for. To get to the point where you embrace that change depends on your sense of ownership and your feeling that you have a choice in the matter.

When my partner proposed making a lifestyle change, I perceived the change as one that was solely his. He owned it entirely, since he had contemplated the idea far longer than I had. My partner and his desire for a new lifestyle were like two forces that had united to become something I had no control over. I felt powerless, because I felt my choices were limited: I could go along with his proposal, or I could walk away from him and this new potential life.

Going cruising eventually became something I embraced— once I invested emotionally in the idea and created my own sense of ownership, and once I developed a sense of control over matters that were important to me and realized that I did indeed have many choices.

I needed to find out what was in this plan for me and to explore what I stood to potentially gain from the cruising life. As I began to explore with my partner the positive and negative implications of the cruising life, I discovered various ways this lifestyle could benefit me. That discovery was pivotal. In this book, you too will learn what aspects of cruising appeal to you as you read about the experiences of the women who went before you.

A supportive partner is key to learning how to deal with an imposed change. In time, I told my partner how few I felt my choices were at first. He assumed I knew that our relationship was far more important to him than pursuing a new life without me. I needed this kind of reassurance—and I would continue to need it for a long time to come.

The following section tells more about the 107 women in the study—those who took a chance and went cruising and how they fared as a group.

## CHOOSING TO CRUISE

When presented with the idea of making a major lifestyle change that would involve moving from land to sea, only 3 of the 107 women I interviewed rejected their partner's proposed change outright and chose not to go cruising. Some of the 104 women who took the risk of embracing the idea were eager participants from the outset; their primary question was "how soon can we leave?" For the vast majority however, the move from land to sea was preceded by a period of contemplation and movement through certain stages (these are discussed in detail in chapter 2). The findings that follow tell you a little more about the women who eventually chose to go cruising and may answer some of your questions about the choices they made (see the appendix for more statistics).

- 80 percent of the women whose partners proposed the cruising life were initially resistant to the idea of living on a boat; of these, 100 percent reported experiencing an "enormous" increase in their overall happiness and life satisfaction because of the change they eventually made

- 65 percent of the women who chose to cruise were between 35 and 55 years of age

- 12 percent had been married for twenty years or more when they first learned their partner harbored the dream of going cruising one day

- 42 percent of the women and their partners were in second marriages

- 78 percent of the women had little or no prior sailing experience

- 75 percent of the women left professional careers to go cruising; 6 percent regretted doing so

- 25 percent were homemakers or had worked only sporadically outside the home

- 5 percent of the women set out cruising with children aboard

- 64 percent of the women lived aboard their vessels for a period of time before going cruising

- 70 percent retained property ashore

- 100 percent of the women who were committed to the concept of cruising at the beginning of my study (but had not yet purchased their vessel and gone cruising) went on to purchase their vessels; 77 percent of those who owned their vessels moved aboard

- 91 percent of the women remained with their partners after they went cruising (and were still with their partners at the time of publication)

- 84 percent of the women who had returned to land at the time of my interview are now cruising again

- o percent of the women let their fear of water or lack of sailing experience prevent them from making the change

Those are some of the facts and figures that define the women in
this study. But behind those statistics are their real-life stories,
many of which you will read about in the pages ahead. You will
see how each woman charted her own course to a new life, each
in her own unique way.

# 2

# A Model for a Lifestyle Change

"How often—even before we began—have we declared a
task "impossible"? And how often have we constructed
a picture of ourselves as being inadequate? A great deal
depends upon the thought patterns we choose and on the
persistence with which we affirm them."

PIERO FERRUCCI

MAKING A MAJOR LIFESTYLE CHANGE IS A
gradual process. I have identified six different stages—from
the initial stage of just talking about the idea to the final stage
of moving back to land—so you can see a model for changing
course to a cruising life.

Exploring the challenges at each stage of the process will
help you move from one stage to the next. It will also enrich the
experience and may lessen the possibility of experiencing a dis-
ruption in your journey.

A typical scenario for this process begins when one partner
reveals his interest in going cruising. Discussions between the
partners may be continuous or intermittent over the months or
years that follow. At some point, the other partner makes a commitment to the concept of living on a boat. Considerable planning and research follow, until the couple purchases their boat.
A period of living aboard often follows, and the transition from
a land life to a cruising life begins in earnest. Then the lines are
cast from the slip and cruising begins. The majority of cruisers
eventually return to land and another period of transition follows.

## WHAT STAGE ARE YOU IN?

As you read this chapter, think about which stage you are currently in. Take a few minutes to jot down your feelings at this point in the process. You may be feeling confused, curious, ambivalent, excited yet cautious, or even overjoyed about changing your life. Whatever your feelings are at this point, you will be heartened by the stories of the women who have been where you are right now.

---

The return to land marks the end of the cruising life and the beginning of new adventures. But in many cases—after the cruising kitty has been replenished, or children have been raised—couples begin talking about going cruising again, and the process of moving from land to sea begins all over again.

The amount of time each stage takes depends on the individuals involved. However, two contributing factors are the noninitiating partner's readiness to move to the next stage and finances.

## STAGE 1. JUST TALKING ABOUT IT

The lifestyle change process is set in motion the moment your partner reveals that he would like to live on a boat and go cruising. Whether you have ongoing discussions about the idea or the topic is shelved indefinitely, your lives will never be the same again: you will find yourself wondering what factors precipitated his cruising dream and what the implications are for you.

For the 107 women I interviewed, the just-talking-about-it stage ranged from 6 months to 17 years or more. Among those I interviewed, the average length of time that elapsed between the just-talking stage and the point at which the noninitiating partner committed to the concept was 4½ years; the median was 2 years. This may seem like a long time to make a decision. But keep in mind that you are making a decision that will profoundly affect your life.

Learning about your partner's dream of going cruising may spark much confusion on your part. His desire to make a major lifestyle change may stem from a need to take stock of his life—and in doing so, he may not like what he's found. There is a natural tendency to wonder, "Am I on that list of things he has outgrown? Am I at the risk of being discarded?" You may find yourself defending a lifestyle that has come to define who you are as an individual and as a couple.

If your resistance to the idea remains strong, your partner may stop talking about his dream. But just because he stops talking about it does not necessarily mean he's abandoned his cruising dream. It's more likely that he is contemplating ways to persuade you to share his dream or, failing that, contemplating ways he might pursue his dream independently.

At this stage, you both need to communicate your thoughts and feelings. Keep talking and keep listening. The more you and your partner talk about the cruising life—and especially the implications for you—the more likely it is that you will both derive tremendous satisfaction from the change you make.

If your partner proposes going cruising at some point in the distant future, you may find yourself half-heartedly agreeing to the concept at the time but then be shocked to learn several years later that his desire to go cruising remains as strong as ever. It is important to be honest. The story of Rebecca and Bob is a valuable lesson.

Rebecca and Bob had vacationed in the Caribbean early in their marriage, and there they discovered a large colony of healthy older people living out their golden years on sailboats. Both thought the cruising lifestyle seemed like a healthy and exciting way to extend their lives, and both agreed that this was the lifestyle they would pursue when their children were independent. At that time, the youngest of their five children was six months old.

In the years that followed, they engaged in intermittent talks about the cruising life—discussing everything from the type of vessel they hoped to own, to the places they planned to visit.

As each child left home Rebecca revisited the plan with Bob, but she became more and more confused about his increasing resistance to the dream they had discussed many years before. Bob eventually confessed that he had agreed to the concept 17 years prior only because he did not believe they would actually move from land to sea.

Rebecca was devastated and felt betrayed. Bob, who was by now enjoying his status as a politician and his financial position, placated Rebecca by assuring her that he would one day be ready to make this change, but he was not ready to do so at the moment.

After four years of watching, Bob become increasingly more involved in civic politics and listening to him scheme about ways to increase their fortunes, Rebecca concluded the time would never be right for Bob—so she embarked on the cruising life without him. Bob was devastated. Rebecca's actions precipitated a crisis in their lives that led them to do much soul-searching about what the future held for them as individuals and as a couple.

Bob and Rebecca eventually reconciled and enjoyed the cruising lifestyle for 15 years before returning to land in their early 70s. Bob said that Rebecca's drastic actions saved his life during those years when he lost sight of what mattered most, first and foremost of which was his life with Rebecca.

My partner first revealed his desire to live on a boat in the fall of 1986. But after that initial revelation, we did not revisit the topic until almost a year later. We then decided to charter a sailboat in the Caribbean to determine if either of us even enjoyed being on a boat! Our discussions spanned a period of seven years, but it was not until the latter part of that period that I was able to make a commitment to the idea. Making that commitment marked the second stage of the process.

## STAGE 2. COMMITTING TO THE CONCEPT

My resistance to going cruising persisted for several years, but my curiosity about this lifestyle remained undiminished. I satisfied my craving for information with cruising and sailing magazines, and I flipped through their glossy pages with a sense of awe: the stories of cruisers and where their boats had taken them fascinated me.

At first I tended to gravitate to the "horror stories," as my partner called them, that recounted in excruciating detail the exploits of individuals who had encountered adversity at sea. My fear was validated by these emotional and graphic testimonials, particularly the stories that were related to weather. I would recount these tales to my partner in the hope that (you guessed it) he would abandon his dream of going cruising.

But eventually, my attitude shifted: I began to analyze each story from an educational perspective, hoping to learn how to avoid a similar fate if we ever went to sea. I essentially stopped reading about cruising as a lifestyle I would never pursue, and I began to absorb knowledge about sailing to prepare myself for life on a boat. When we did go on offshore passages, some of those stories of doom became textbooks for disaster prevention.

At some point in your journey, the concept of living on a

boat may take hold and you'll find yourself yearning to learn more about this lifestyle. As you gain more knowledge, you will be able to formulate your own picture of cruising and imagine yourself living on the water. Some ways you can satisfy your quest for knowledge include

- reading books and magazines that focus on sailing and cruising

- talking extensively with your partner about cruising

- taking sailing courses on boat handling, weather, provisioning, safety, and navigation (many women take these on their own, but some take them with their partners)

- researching product information on equipment that you would consider installing on your boat

- scanning sailboat ads in magazines and taking excursions with your partner to search for your perfect boat

For Beth, age 42, seeing more of the cruising life in magazines helped her to shift her dreams to the water. "We'd always wanted to buy a piece of land and be self-sufficient—grow our own vegetables, raise a few chickens," she said. "Then he started buying sailing magazines; he'd bring them home and try to talk me into looking at them. But I refused. I had my *Harrowsmith* and *Mother Earth News* magazines. Then one day, I picked one up: before I knew it, an hour had passed. I was captivated by pictures of places I'd always dreamed of visiting but had resigned myself to never seeing. We could just never afford to travel to those places. It took me a while, but one day I realized I could see all these places if I lived on a boat. That was it: I was sold."

Many women found that as their knowledge about cruising increased, so too did their confidence. And with increased confidence came a stronger comfort level about making a shift to living on the water.

# STAGE 3. PURCHASING THE BOAT

The purchase of your boat represents a concrete commitment to the cruising life. Going cruising is no longer an abstract dream that may or may not come to fruition. But as soon as you buy your boat, you will have more questions to answer: How will the vessel be equipped? What cargo is essential and what can we leave behind? When will our boat become our full-time home?

## A MUTUAL CHOICE

In many cases, the initiating partner has spent several years dreaming about the type of vessel he hopes to someday purchase. But when your search begins together in earnest, it does not preclude looking at new vessels at boat shows, used boats at dockside, and the occasional trek through hayfields to old barns! Many couples don't have a specific model in mind, so they set out to look at just about anything that floats. Over time they develop a list of their wants and needs.

Your active involvement in selecting your boat will largely determine the extent to which you feel like an equal partner in this lifestyle change. The majority of women I interviewed were active participants in selecting their boats and the choice of boat was often contingent on their satisfaction with a particular vessel. In instances where the woman was not involved in the selection, or when the boat was previously owned by her partner, the woman was more apt to perceive that boat as *his* boat rather than *our* boat. I am not suggesting that women have the ultimate say in choosing a boat, but I am advocating for an equal partnership in all decisions.

In many cases a woman's intuition about a particular vessel is a vital component of the selection process. If her partner heeds it, she will more often than not become emotionally invested in the cruising life the moment she feels a particular boat is perfect for their new life. I was lucky to have a partner who understood this.

---

### FINDING *BEEDAHBUN* AND *RED WITCH*

Several years ago my partner and I drove north of Toronto on a cold and rainy day to look into chartering a trawler for a few weeks. We made inquiries at the first marina we came to that had access to Georgian Bay, and we were informed that the chartering of motor vessels had ceased several years ago. We were told that it was too expensive and not many people were interested.

"It's too bad you're not looking to buy something," said Harry, the owner of the marina. "The owner of one of the nicest boats on the Bay has just decided to sell, and the price is darn good." After determining that Harry had no vested interest in the sale of any boat in his complex, I asked if we could see the boat.

Meanwhile, my partner was wandering up and down the docks looking at the boats gently rocking in their slips. I signaled to him, and he joined Harry and me as we made our way through a dilapidated boathouse that looked as though it would crumble at any moment. Then I saw her. She had a royal-blue hull that illuminated her glossy hand- and toenails, and her spacious aft deck invited us to dance. I was awestruck by such a fine

piece of craftsmanship—even though I had nothing to compare her to. I asked Harry what the asking price was and turned
to my partner and whispered, "This is the boat. We've got to
buy her!" I cannot explain why I sensed this particular boat
was for us; I simply knew. And so began our relationship with
*Red Witch*, a classic wooden boat that we cruise on Georgian Bay
during the summer.

My partner trusted my intuition with *Red Witch* and again
several years later when we spotted *Beedahbun*, our motor sailor.
When asked how we came to acquire our boats, my partner
will state unequivocally that my intuition and instant attraction
for these boats was the most important criterion. He trusted my
intuition, and he knew that if I was enamored with the boat, I'd
be more likely to consider the boat our boat rather than his boat.
He was right.

---

SHARING THE DECISIONS OF REFITTING AND REFURBISHING
It is essential that you are actively involved in all aspects of decision making in any refitting or refurbishing you do. You may not
be interested in (or capable of) participating in the actual refit, but
you must have a voice in how things are done. Lorraine, age 34,
learned this lesson while she worked full time in Washington
and her partner refit their boat over 2,000 miles away in Hawaii.

*We flew to Hawaii, where we found a boat we both loved. But it
needed lots of work. So [my partner] stayed in Hawaii to work on the
boat and I returned to Washington. We agreed that I would continue to
work until he finished the boat, and I would track down and ship supplies he couldn't get in Hawaii.*

*It took nine months for him to complete the refit. When I finally flew
to Hawaii to join him, I felt like an outsider on his boat: he had decided*

*on the layout of the galley and aft cabin; he had decided what would go where; he had made decisions about specific pieces of equipment that I didn't necessarily agree with.*

*People would come by and ooh and ah over his workmanship. I had spent the last nine months tracking down supplies, bundling them up, and arranging them to be shipped: there was no appreciation for that aspect of things. I did not feel like this was our boat—and it wasn't. It was his boat, refitted according to his ideas.*

*If I did it all over again, I would be more actively involved in the decision making. I'd insist that the plans be faxed to me so we could discuss things over the phone. I'd factor into our budget the cost of my flying over to Hawaii a couple of times to see how things were going and to have more involvement.*

As you search for your boat and do the necessary refitting, pay particular attention to the areas of the vessel where you expect to spend significant portions of your time. Whether it's the galley or the engine room, you must have a voice in the layout and the choice of equipment.

When we were equipping *Beedahbun* for living aboard and cruising, I suggested we convert one of the hanging closets to a pantry with shelves. If I had simply asked my partner to install shelves, I might have ended up with shelves that were not able to accommodate the items I planned to store in that space. I specified the articles I planned to store there (including a blender, pressure cooker, and a stewing pot), and I got exactly what I wanted because I was an active participant in the project.

Many women who are not as familiar with sailboats as their partners are often reluctant to assert their opinions and preferences. But if you take this stance, you will always find yourself acquiescing to your partner's ideas and preferences.

# STAGE 4. LIVING ABOARD

Once they have purchased a boat, many couples move aboard and live in a slip at a well-equipped marina while they make the gradual transition from land to sea. Most continue to work in their chosen fields during this time, to increase the cruising kitty.

Many women found this liveaboard period to be a time of transition and adaptation, and some found it to be a stressful time. Adjusting to a new kind of space was a key factor.

For some women, their most anxious time was before they actually moved on board. Much of the uncertainty stemmed from not knowing how they would enjoy living in a small, confined space with their partner. But many women were surprised to discover how much they enjoyed living in a small space—a space where household chores took a fraction of the time, compared to their land-based homes.

"I can have the place cleaned and organized in less than twenty minutes. The rest of the time is my own to read, sketch, walk the boardwalk, or sit on deck and watch the gulls," said Jackie, age 39.

My experience was similar. On *Beedahbun*, we have fewer material possessions than we do in our land-based home, but our quality of life has not been compromised in the least. On the contrary, less has come to mean more. There are fewer cupboards to keep tidy, less linen to fold, fewer pots and pans to maneuver, and more time to explore and discover new skills. I also derive a tremendous sense of accomplishment from knowing I can live comfortably with less.

> "**I** can have the place cleaned and organized in less than twenty minutes. The rest of the time is my own to read, sketch, walk the boardwalk, or sit on deck and watch the gulls."
>
> JACKIE

For some, this stage was stressful, for it was a time of having one foot in each of two different worlds. If you and your partner continue your land-based careers and other activities, you may require more space than you have on board for wardrobes and leisure equipment. You will have to reduce your wardrobes and equipment or find a storage space elsewhere. Some women converted the back seats and trunks of their cars to closets; others stored several changes of clothing at their offices; some used the lockers at their fitness facility to store a few outfits.

If you plan to keep your land-based home and rent it out when you move on board, you may be able to negotiate access to a room that will serve as your storage space. Some cruisers house a telephone with a silent ringer and an answering service in that room, so they can retrieve messages from around the world. This way, they do not have to inconvenience those who are residing in their home.

If you keep a separate room in your house, you might consider installing a separate entrance, which will allow you unrestricted access to that room. Often, a friend or family member who lives in the area will allow you unrestricted access to a storage room in their home. Another option, albeit a less preferred one due to cost, is to rent an on-land storage space that is accessible 24 hours a day.

In addition to becoming familiar with your vessel and adjusting to living in a smaller space, you and your partner will also invest considerable time and money selecting equipment, installing it, and becoming familiar with your boat's many systems.

You and your partner can also discover new ways of living together and relating to one another in a more intimate environment. This stage is a time when you can catch your breath, take stock of how far you have come, and celebrate this exciting step that brings you closer to your cruising dream.

# STAGE 5. LIVING ABOARD AND CRUISING

If you're readying to cast your lines from a dock that served as a transitional place, you and your partner are about to experience the cruising life in its purest sense. This is the stage when your theoretical and vicarious knowledge is integrated with first-hand experience. It is also the stage that many women characterize as one of "extreme highs" and "extreme lows." An overnight passage under a full moon on calm seas is romantic and unforgettable; equally unforgettable is a passage of gale-force winds, converging waves and a horizon nowhere in sight for days on end!

Kim and Allen, both in their early 40s, had never experienced an overnight sail. They spent three months learning to sail their vessel on Lake Ontario before beginning a three-month journey down the Intracoastal Waterway (ICW). Kim described this six-month period as involving "a steep learning curve and a time of consolidation." They made their first overnight crossing to the Bahamas with a flotilla (a group of boats that travel together on specific passages). Kim described her first overnight passage this way.

*Neither of us had any idea what to expect. We'd been told that crossing the Gulf Stream [to the Bahamas] could be a wild time but the ocean was like glass. We ended up motoring for most of the passage.*

*I don't remember ever seeing stars as bright as the ones that scattered the skies that night. At one point I looked over the stern and saw streaks of green lights trailing after us and I realized that this is what people refer to as phosphorescence. It was almost magical.*

*Neither of us slept that night. We were too excited!*

The majority of women I interviewed spent varying lengths of time coastal cruising or cruising down the ICW prior to embarking on overnight passages of any duration. This enabled them and their partners to become more familiar with their vessels, and to experience varying sailing conditions while in close proximity to land. A few women, whose partners were more experienced sailors, chose to fly between ports and let their partners make the passage with crew until such time as the women were comfortable making the passages themselves.

> **"If you don't feel ready to make a passage, don't!"**
>
> DONNA

Donna, who had never sailed out of sight of land, offered this advice to women who are not comfortable making a long passage.

*If you don't feel ready to make a passage, don't! There are all kinds of people out there who are looking for offshore sailing experience. [My partner] and I agreed from the outset that I would not make any passage that I was not comfortable making. He had lots of friends who were experienced sailors and wanted to do an offshore passage.*

*At one point I wasn't comfortable making the seven-day passage to Bermuda even though [by then] I had done one- to two-day passages. [My partner] respected my decision.*

Donna eventually chose to make the first of many multiday passages with her partner. Currently, she and her partner are readying for their first transatlantic crossing that they'll undertake with three additional crew members on board.

The length of time the women in my study cruised ranged from ten months to over twenty years. Some women and their partners took one- and two-year sabbaticals after which they returned to land-based professions—all with the plan to one day cruise for longer durations. Several women made a commitment to the cruising lifestyle for a specific duration after which they retained the right to choose to continue cruising or to return to land. Others set out with no predetermined time frame; finances and their enjoyment of the lifestyle would dictate when they returned to land. And, in a few rare instances, the women discovered that they enjoyed the cruising life far more than their initiating partners! In these instances the women continued to live aboard their vessels and their partners resumed life on land, independently.

Whether you and your partner take a one-year sabbatical to go cruising or set off for an undefined period of time, this stage of your lifestyle change is bound to change how you feel about yourself, your partner, your relationship, and life in general. You will master new skills, meet new people, see new places, derive unexpected pleasure from a simpler life, and develop a deeper appreciation for the beauty of the earth.

Jen's closing remarks during our interview illuminate the joy of cruising best of all.

*It would have been so easy for me to choose not to go cruising. [My partner] and I weren't married, we didn't have children, I had a career I loved, a circle of friends I adored, and no shortage of things to do on land. I thought to myself [when he suggested we go cruising] there is no way that lifestyle [cruising] can compete.*

> "**I** am a better person for making this change and my partner and I are a happier couple."
>
> JEN

*But I have to tell you, when I took the helm on our first overnight passage and the moon was full and the ocean was like a pond, I felt more in touch with a higher power than I can explain. Something happened out there that I can't explain.*

*I am a better person for making this change and my partner and I are a happier couple.*

# STAGE 6. BACK ON LAND

Coming back to land is yet another odyssey of change. The women I interviewed all reported that returning to land life evoked feelings of resistance, ambivalence, and/or a great sense of loss—not unlike the feelings they experienced in the earliest stages of contemplating life on a boat.

Some women reported the transition back to land to be *more* challenging than their move on board: the dizzying pace of land life contrasted drastically with the tranquility of life on the water, and consumer excessiveness was a stark reminder of the economic imbalances throughout the world.

"I'll never forget going to the supermarket for the first time after we returned," said Barb, age 54. "We had become accustomed to having so few items from which to choose, and in many of the countries there were no choices. [Back on land] I was overwhelmed with a sense of extravagance. I felt embarrassed. I wondered why we needed to have so much when in so many parts of the world people have so little and do so well."

The sixth stage is not necessarily the final stage of the cruising life: for most, it's a time for reflection, consolidation, celebration, and new beginnings. All but one woman hoped to resume the cruising life again in the future.

Most returned to land to restock the cruising kitty; some returned because their sabbaticals had ended; for a few women, returning to land marked the end of cruising with one partner and the beginning of life on a boat alone or with another partner, after a period of consolidation on land. But these women had one thing in common: the cruising lifestyle had forever changed them.

As I write this book, most—84 percent—of the women who were back on land at the time of my study have resumed life on a boat. All of them reported a greater degree of readiness for the cruising life the second time around—and all welcomed the return to a simpler, more tranquil life.

The story of Carol, who sailed with her husband Joe for two years, illustrates how the first cruise can prepare you for a second chance at a life on the water. It was Joe's idea initially to go cruising; Carol did not share his love of sailing. But she felt compelled to support his dream, for fear that he might otherwise pursue it on his own.

Their time at sea was, in Carol's words, "a nightmare." She was plagued with seasickness, terrified of the water, and counted the days until they would return to land. Their plan was to return in two years and build a dream house in the mountains, but Joe confessed that he had no real intention of ever living in the mountains. However, he conceded that he had promised they would return to land in two years' time, and he made good on that promise.

The plans for a dream home had lost their luster, so they purchased a condominium on a lake and began to see if they could agree on a lifestyle that was mutually beneficial for them both.

Joe and Carol are currently cruising in the South Pacific, and they are thoroughly enjoying their cruising lifestyle. Of her second time around, Carol says, "I am here because I have chosen to be here—not because I feel I have to be." This is their story, as recounted by Carol on the eve of their departure for their second cruise.

*I knew I hadn't given the cruising life a fair shake. I refused to read anything that Joe gave me. I didn't want to learn how to sail the boat. I went along for all the wrong reasons, but I didn't feel I had a choice: I thought he would go without me. When I look back, it's a miracle our marriage survived.*

*It's not like I had a career that was keeping me on land. I didn't even have any special hobbies or interests. To be honest, I didn't have a better plan. When we returned to land, I decided to reflect on our experience and try to make sense of it.*

*I confessed that I had never liked the boat. Joe had no idea I felt this way. I decided to see a therapist, to trace the roots of my fear of the water. Joe was completely supportive of this and at one point came along to several sessions. He discovered stuff about himself and me, about us. The therapist talked about the importance of an equal partnership in any plan. We realized that although we had an equal partnership on land, this was not the case with the decision to go cruising—nor did I feel like an equal partner on the boat.*

> "**I** am here because I have chosen to be here—not because I feel I have to be."
>
> CAROL

*We're getting ready to go cruising again in three months. This time I'm really keen on going. I've taken sailing lessons on my own. I found a course on navigation fascinating, and I want to put my new skills to work. We sold the old boat and found one we're both nuts about. We're going to spend the summer getting acquainted with her and settling in. If I'm not ready to sail south before the winter, Joe is OK about that.*

*The difference this time? I have a choice. I know Joe won't leave without me. I'm committed to the concept and we have talked about what I potentially have to gain from this lifestyle. Before it was all about what Joe wanted. Now it's about what I want and need too.*

Carol and Joe have kept their condominium. They'll return to it from time to time when they need a reprieve from life afloat.

Many couples choose to retain a land base in anticipation of a future date when they will return to land. And some choose to alternate their time on the boat with time spent on land. Dawn and Patrick are one such couple.

*We really weren't sure if we'd like living on a boat full time. Patrick wasn't certain he'd enjoy retirement and I wanted a fallback just in case we missed our land life. We cruised for fifteen months initially, then decided to put the boat up [on land] in Turkey and return home for a few months. It's not that we didn't like living aboard: we simply wanted to go back to land for a while. After four months on land we were eager to return to the boat. There's no doubt about it: the cruising life is wonderful. But I like the variety that comes with doing both.*

*We were just home again for three months. We're thinking that eventually we'll do six months on and six months off.*

Whether you choose to cruise full time or part time, you can learn more about the advantages and disadvantages of various options in chapter 7.

# 3

# The Most Common Concerns

"Life shrinks or expands in proportion to one's
courage."

ANAÏS NIN

JOAN, AGE 53, HAD KNOWN HER PARTNER
since childhood. Still, his dream of going cruising came as a total surprise. "After he told me that cruising was something he'd
dreamed of doing since he was a child, I racked my brain trying
to remember if he had ever so much as alluded to it," she said.
"He later told me that he had never mentioned it before because
it seemed highly unlikely that such a thing could ever happen!"

Joan was not alone. Upon hearing of their partner's desire to
make a major lifestyle change, the majority of women responded with feelings of shock, disbelief, and even ambivalence.
But tremors of excitement and a growing sense of curiosity soon
crept in, and many found themselves considering the change
and making a mental inventory of how cruising would impact
their lives. Maybe you have already started your own inventory.

As you learn more about cruising boats, you will see that
technology has made life on boats safer and more comfortable.
Living on board no longer has to simulate a rained-out camping
trip, replete with sopping-wet sleeping bags and a diet of

canned food. Today's cruisers can bed down in queen-size berths with cotton sheets and a duvet. Modern galleys enable cruisers to prepare gourmet meals. And many cruisers carry a well-stocked wine cellar in their sole.

The ability to live comfortably on a boat is not the only modern-day enticement. Navigation, which once required mathematical prowess and skill with a sextant, has been made less complicated with global satellite positioning technology: the GPS is a handheld, battery-operated navigational instrument that's as easy to operate as a VCR. Your likelihood of unexpectedly encountering heavy weather has been decreased significantly; onboard computers, weather fax, and round-the-clock radio weather broadcasts will help you learn what weather lies ahead. Offshore telecommunications systems have never been more reliable, and it is now possible to establish telephone contact with land-based friends and family from just about anywhere in the world. With the right equipment, you can also send and receive e-mail from your boat in minutes. Indeed, cruising has never been easier, safer, or more enjoyable.

Regardless of the technological advances that have made cruising more attractive to more people, there are still many concerns you are likely to have—about your personal safety at sea and how this new lifestyle will affect your career, your interpersonal relationships, and your dreams and aspirations. The following issues were the most common concerns among the women in my study:

- having little or no sailing experience

- loss of proximity to family and friends

- safety

- giving up careers and jobs

- finances

- disappointing their partners (if they are unable to go through with the lifestyle change)

## SAILING EXPERIENCE

If you have little or no prior sailing experience, you are bound to feel anxious about going cruising. But keep in mind that 78 percent of the women I interviewed had little or no prior sailing experience. If your partner's sailing experience parallels your own, then you will be starting out on an equal footing: you can learn together and reinforce each other's achievements. But if you perceive your partner's skills as superior to your own skills, you may feel intimidated.

Everybody starts somewhere: with practice and your partner's support, you can develop your own skill set. There are many good sailing schools, some of which are designed exclusively for women. Some of the women in my study took classes with their partners, and some went to school on their own. Sailing school may open up a new world to you. There are courses on boat handling, navigation, provisioning, engine maintenance, and safety—and your education doesn't stop when you set sail, for you will never stop developing your skills further.

Interpersonal dynamics with your partner can enhance or inhibit your learning experiences. This is the story of Caroline, age 56.

*The more confident I became, the more involved I tried to become. But the more critical he became of my efforts. It was as though he really didn't want me to know as much as he did. Before we left he told me I needed to know all kinds of things. He bought me a book on how to tie knots. I didn't have much interest in tying knots before we moved on the boat, but once on board, I'd practice. The best times were when I was on watch at night. He'd relieve me and I'd try to show him what I'd learned. But he wasn't interested in the least: I think that's because he couldn't tie those knots himself!*

**"I** didn't have much interest in tying knots before we moved on the boat, but once on board, I'd practice."

C A R O L I N E

Some men feel threatened by their partner's achievements, and they gain a sense of power from perpetuating her dependency rather than encouraging her learning efforts. Women in this situation fail to develop self-confidence and they become increasingly demoralized and often assume a passive role. The cruising lifestyle becomes one that she endures until they return to land. Both partners often blame the nature of the cruising life—when in fact their problems began long before they ever left land.

The best gauge for predicting how supportive your partner will be in your efforts to become a more competent sailor is to consider how supportive he has been of other learning projects you undertook on land. If he cheered you on and encouraged you, then he is likely to do the same on a boat. But if he has undermined your learning efforts on land, don't expect any less of this at sea.

## PROXIMITY TO FAMILY

In recent years, more couples are choosing to cruise with young children. However, the majority of couples set sail without children aboard. A paramount concern for the women in my study was not being readily accessible to their adult children, their grandchildren, and their aging parents—especially in the case of an emergency.

### BEING CREATIVE ABOUT COMMUNICATING

Concerns about proximity to family were lessened considerably for women who developed creative means for communicating with their family.

Most waited until they arrived in port to access telephones and collect and send mail. One woman explained how she would send letters home with virtual strangers she met in different ports; they would agree to post her letters when they arrived back in the United States. Still others described the reward of locating a working telephone on a remote island. On their wanderings, they'd barter for supplies and learn from the locals about an island's best-kept secrets.

Maintaining written contact with friends and family is easy to do, but having immediate contact with those on land depends on the type of telecommunications equipment you have on board. If your vessel is equipped with a ham and/or single-side band (SSB) radio, you will be able to establish a system for regular contact with family and friends ashore. These high-frequency radios transmit and receive over long distances.

Ham and SSB radio continues to be the telecommunications system of choice for most cruisers, in part because the equipment is more available than any other and therefore has led to the establishment of "cruising nets" that most cruisers have come to depend on. Cruising nets are essentially party lines to which cruisers tune their radios at predesignated times to chat. These modes of communication have also, until recently, been far less expensive than other options.

Offshore communications options are more numerous today

than they were only a few years ago. Satellite and cellular telephone systems—once far beyond the average cruiser's budget—have become more affordable and, in many instances, more reliable. Consequently, family and friends are hardly more than a phone call away. It may be an expensive phone call, but one you can both resort to when time is of the essence.

Several women set a goal of learning how to transmit on SSB and/or ham radios. Their confidence soared—both because they experienced a sense of achievement and because this liberated them from being dependent on their partner to do the transmissions.

> **"My advice to any woman going cruising is to buy a computer and learn how to use it."**
>
> MARY

Computers are becoming an increasingly popular way for cruisers to keep in touch with family and friends. I would advise you to buy your computer and know how to use it to send and receive e-mail *before* you leave land. This includes not only learning how to use the computer but learning how to transmit e-mail via your SSB, ham radio, or onboard cellular telephone system. If you are planning to stay in one place for any length of time, it's possible to arrange for a local cellular number as well as an Internet service provider (ISP), which can reduce transmission costs substantially. The addition of a digital camera will even enable you to transmit photographs!

If you don't have the capacity to send and receive e-mail from your boat, you can always take your laptop ashore and access a telephone line. And if a computer simply isn't in your budget, look for a cyber café where you can send and receive e-mail. They're popping up almost everywhere, including on some of the most remote islands.

Mary, age 74, found that learning to operate a computer made a huge difference and helped her feel more connected to her grandchildren.

*We've been cruising for twenty years now. Every day I'm confronted with new challenges, and on most days, I learn something that I didn't know the day before. Computers weren't the "in" thing when we lived on land. The kids gave us a computer for Christmas last year, and I remember thinking, "What does a woman my age need a computer for?" When we arrived in Georgetown, I met a woman on a boat who was giving computer lessons. I thought, "I've got nothing better to do and this seems like a good way to meet a few more people." My kids were astonished when they received the first e-mails I sent. We're in touch a couple times a week now: it's made all the difference in the world. I feel more connected to my grandchildren. This was a real worry for me before we left. My advice to any woman going cruising is to buy a computer and learn how to use it.*

## ENRICHING THE LIVES OF YOUR GRANDCHILDREN

One of the most difficult aspects of cruising for many women is not having regular involvement with their young grandchildren. But while the cruising life may prevent you from having day-to-day involvement in their lives, you have a great potential to enrich their lives by sharing your cruising adventures with them.

> **"H**ow many grandparents get that kind of opportunity, to share such an unforgettable experience and adventure with their grandchildren? . . . We were close on land, but we developed a special bond at sea that has endured."
>
> ELLIE

Children delight in getting letters and postcards from faraway, exotic places—especially when those postcards are addressed to them personally! Older children often begin collecting stamps. And inviting grandchildren, nieces, and nephews to experience the cruising life will give them memories that will last a lifetime. Imagine an 8-year-old child taking his shell collection to school and describing how he and his grandmother waited for the tide to recede early one morning so they could comb the beach. Imagine a 14-year-old girl deciding that she wants to become a marine biologist because she was so fascinated by the underwater sea life she saw with her grandfather.

And don't discount the idea of taking a grandchild or two along for a portion of your journey. Ellie, the 59-year-old grandmother of Jen, age 12, arranged for her granddaughter to come on a transatlantic crossing. "How many grandparents get that kind of opportunity, to share such an unforgettable experience and adventure with their grandchildren?" said Ellie. "We were close on land, but we developed a special bond at sea that has endured."

## SAFETY

Safety is high on the cruising woman's list of concerns. But as you prepare to go cruising, you will equip yourself with knowledge and know-how, so you will feel capable and confident of dealing with the safety situations you will face. Among cruising women, the most common concerns about safety pertain to three areas: severe weather; the integrity of a vessel; and the fear of a partner becoming disabled or dying at sea. Fewer than 6 percent of the women interviewed experienced severe weather conditions or a partner becoming disabled. All agreed that their experiences could have been prevented.

Many women wonder how small boats can withstand large ocean waves—and whether the crew will live to tell the story. I still marvel at the physics that enable a sailboat to immediately right itself in the unlikely event of a knockdown, in which a strong, sudden gust of wind knocks a boat on its side. Offshore cruising boats are built to endure what marine architects consider the average of the worst of conditions, or just about any heavy weather. And seasoned cruisers will tell you that the crew is far more likely to give up the boat in the worst conditions than the boat is likely to give up the crew. The seaworthiness of your vessel very much depends on the care you and your partner take in maintaining it and on your understanding of its systems. Knowing, for example, where the emergency bilge pump is stored and how to operate it in the event the boat is taking on water can make all the difference in keeping your vessel afloat and your nerves from fraying.

You can control the likelihood of being caught unprepared in extreme weather. By choosing appropriate weather windows, listening carefully to daily weather broadcasts, and carefully analyzing predicted weather patterns, you greatly reduce the likelihood of being caught unprepared in adverse weather. You can also choose not to cruise during the cyclone or hurricane seasons. Many cruisers head south of the hurricane belt to sit out the season. Still others put their vessels on land and return to a land base for a few months each year.

Women who have cruised for many years have some sage advice: don't put schedules and deadlines before safety. If the weather is questionable, wait for a better weather window before you depart for the next port.

Concern about your partner's safety, and how a mishap would affect you both, is natural. This concern is especially acute for women who are not confident in their ability to singlehand their boats. Learning to sail your vessel without your partner's participation should rank high on your list of skills to learn. You will not only feel less vulnerable; your partner will also feel less stressed knowing that in an emergency you can manage the helm.

Agreeing on basic safety practices before you sail off will ultimately make for a less stressful cruise. For example, a standard safety practice on many boats is that all crew must wear life vests and safety harnesses when on deck from dusk to dawn. A few women said their partners refused to wear safety harnesses (which tether you to your boat) during their nighttime watches. The concern of these women is well founded: prudent sailors know that the chances of retrieving someone who falls into the sea after dark are slim.

Kerri, age 60, had a partner who refused to wear a safety harness under any conditions. "I'm supposed to sleep while he's on watch, but instead I lie in my bunk and pray that he won't fall overboard, knowing that I probably won't hear him if he does," she said. The stress and exhaustion that resulted prompted Kerri to return to land after a lengthy offshore voyage. She remained there until her partner agreed to wear a safety harness when he was alone on deck at night.

It's important to know how to singlehand your boat; it's also important to know what to do in an emergency if your partner becomes disabled. Mary, age 29, had to handle such an emergency situation; but events might have been different had she and her partner waited for a better weather window. This is her story.

*We were three days out of Hawaii when I became so seasick I couldn't move from my bunk. The seas were enormous and confused: I was so afraid that I wouldn't leave my bunk—even if I could have. [My partner] was exhausted from being at the helm nonstop. He kept saying the weather would clear a day or two after we left, but it just got worse. I had wanted to remain in port until the weather cleared, but he was anxious to get underway. I remember thinking, "Why are we hurrying?"*

*I was lying in my bunk on the fifth night out thinking that death would be a relief. All of a sudden the boat veered to starboard and I heard an awful bang. I crawled up the companionway and looked out to see [my partner] slumped over in the cockpit. He'd been knocked unconscious by the boom. I was sure he was dead.*

*I put out a call on the SSB [single-sideband radio] for emergency assistance. We were rescued the next morning. The boat was lost. Dick had suffered a fractured skull and a broken arm, and I was in hospital with dehydration for five days.*

*What would I do differently if I was in the same situation? Well, I wouldn't be in the same situation. I would have insisted we wait for better weather.*

One safety procedure you and your partner should make a point of perfecting whether you're day sailors or cruisers is the "crew-overboard" drill. There are variations of the drill, but all have a common goal: get the person who has fallen into the water back into the boat as quickly as possible. And don't just *read* about the crew-overboard drill: *practice it routinely.*

If your partner turns a deaf ear to your concerns and takes risks that jeopardize both your lives, you will have difficulty trusting his judgment. Mutual trust and respect underlie the high degree of interdependency that is inherent in the cruising life. Without that, you might both be at risk.

Fears about your safety are natural, and overcoming those fears is an evolving process aided by your increased experience and skill. Practical suggestions for managing fear are discussed in chapter 5.

## WHAT ABOUT MY CAREER?

One of my primary concerns about going cruising was the loss of my career. I had developed a fulfilling and successful consulting practice, and I thrived on my work. My fear of losing a career that had come to define me as a person was partly what motivated me to conduct this study.

I predicted that women who had fulfilling careers would be very reluctant to sacrifice them, and I expected those who had left careers to urge me not to abandon mine. I planned to use these findings as more ammunition for my resistance to making a change.

But I never found those responses. I was astonished at how few women were concerned about relinquishing their careers or, in the case of those who took sabbaticals, compromising their opportunities for promotions. In fact, the vast majority were not! A few women were mildly concerned that technological advancements would make their skills obsolete should they return to their respective fields, and a few women expressed ambivalence about relinquishing their place on the corporate ladder, after having worked so long to get there. The majority of women expressed confidence in their ability to find work that would sustain them, when and if this was necessary. Only one woman was not prepared to sacrifice a career she loved for a lifestyle that held no attraction for her.

Those who felt ambivalent about leaving a career found that their feelings diminished once they were actually immersed in the cruising lifestyle and able to develop a sense of themselves independent of their careers. "In the past, my self-esteem was tied to my work," said one woman. "I didn't think I was anyone without my work. As I've become more self-confident in this environment, I've discovered that I don't need a job to define who I am."

One of the most revealing passages on careers was from Meryl, a 58-year-old vice president of a large marketing firm who was preparing to set sail indefinitely with her partner. Neither she nor her partner Bart had any sailing experience.

*Being at the top is not all it's made out to be. As a woman, do I feel especially fortunate to have achieved such status? Not particularly. I sure have a better understanding of how stressful it must have been for my husband when he was in the corporate world: you spend half your time worrying about who's being groomed to replace you, and you know it's just a matter of time before that happens. And then what? The bottom line is, it's just a job. So when he said, "What do you think about selling everything and sailing south?" I panicked for a moment. I said, "We've never sailed!" And he said, "We'll learn!" He was right. And you know what? We've never had so much fun together: reading books, trying to decide what kind of boat we want, going to boat shows.*

Meryl and Bart had a two-year plan, during which time Meryl was to ease out of her management position. Within six months they found their perfect boat. The house they thought would take two years to sell was listed and sold in seven days. They spent the summer sailing the Great Lakes before heading south on the Intracoastal Waterway to Florida. I hear from Meryl periodically. "People at work said I wouldn't last a day," she wrote. "They said I was too high strung to lounge around a boat. Well, I wouldn't call what I do lounging. There's never an end to things that need to be done. They'd be shocked to hear I've taken up painting. Bart thinks I'm the next Monet. I'm having a ball!"

Many cruising women reported how they discovered latent talents. Some developed photography skills; some became seamstresses; some became writers and have published their work in cruising magazines; some even wrote books. Offshore cooking schools in France and Italy enticed a few women; and in addition to enhancing their repertoire of culinary skills, they've also become proficient in a second language.

Jan, age 37, had longed to learn more about photography since her teens. Cruising gave her a chance to learn. "I take my camera everywhere," she said. "The best shots usually happen when you least expect it so you've got to have your camera ready and with you at all times. I wouldn't have dreamed of taking my camera everywhere with me when we were land based. Now it's like an appendage and I can't imagine leaving the boat without it."

Every woman who has embarked on the cruising life reported learning practical skills and/or developing creative talents that she would not have developed on land—from writing poetry, to bleeding a diesel engine, to making jewelry from shells. These skills may not relate to future career interests. But for many they instill a level of self-confidence that can only enhance whatever career opportunities these women pursue over the next horizon.

## FINANCES

How much does the cruising lifestyle cost and how do couples finance their cruising dream? The answers are as individual as cruisers are. In this section I give you an idea of sample budgets and factors that will affect your spending; how cruisers manage their lives so they can afford to go cruising; and advice from cruising women on ways you and your partner can consider managing your funds together.

### SAMPLE BUDGETS
The costs of the cruising lifestyle can vary drastically, depending on your individual tastes and preferences. I have talked with cruisers whose monthly budgets ranged from as little as $250 a month to as high as $3,000 a month and more (all figures are in U.S. currency). The most commonly stated figure is $1,500 a month, or $18,000 a year.

Most cruisers agree that if you have more, you tend to spend more. And many cruisers report that a whole lot of living can be

had for not a whole lot of money. There is truth in both state-
ments. At various times in our life together, my partner and I
have lived on a lot and lived on a little; some of our most memorable times have been the ones when we had little money but
a lot of imagination.

Annie Hill, author of *Voyaging on a Small Income*, and her husband Peter are living proof that you don't need to be rich to
enjoy the cruising life. These full-time cruisers choose to live
modestly on what many would consider to be a subsistence income of about $2,200 a year. The Hills built their 34-foot sail-
ing dory, *Badger*, and they have cruised the world's waterways
for more than fifteen years. They equate independence with simplicity and derive considerable satisfaction from living on a very
small income.

The Hills's budget may not be one you or I would choose,
but it is a testament to the less-is-better philosophy that some
people are seeking. However, I would caution you to determine
just how small a budget you can happily exist on.

If you feel chronically deprived as a consequence of existing
on a very limited budget, you may become depressed and question whether the cruising life is for you. One of the reasons you
are considering embracing this unique lifestyle is to play tourist
in countries that you have long dreamed of exploring. One of
the attractions of cruising is travel to faraway, exotic places—
places where you will want to sample local cuisine, rent a vehicle to tour the island, take in local attractions, perhaps take
language classes, and buy a souvenir or two. You haven't come
all this way to sit at anchor and gaze longingly at the shore! If
your budget is so limited that you cannot afford to do these
types of things, at least some of the time, you may eventually
find yourself wondering why you are living a lifestyle that
promised so much and delivered so little.

I urge would-be cruisers to factor into their budgets generous funds for onshore exploring. If you don't spend your allocated funds at one destination, you will have no difficulty doubling your indulgences further along the way. And practically speaking, the adage "err on the side of caution" could not be truer when it comes to formulating a cruising budget: plan to live on more rather than less. This way, you will have a bit of wiggle room for the unexpected as well as for the occasional indulgence.

*Factors that Affect Your Budget*

The cruising lifestyle may cost more or less than your land-based lifestyle, depending on a number of variables that include (but are not limited to) the following:

- your anticipated cruising grounds and the length of time you expect to remain there (some countries, such as the Dominican Republic, are very inexpensive; some islands, such as the British Virgin Islands, are quite expensive)

- whether or not you will continue making mortgage payments on your vessel and/or a property ashore

- whether or not you will be paying to store possessions on land

- whether or not you will be paying annual insurance premiums (home, boat, auto, health, life, etc.)

- the number of annual trips you plan to make back to the mainland

- whether or not you will be paying the airfare for adult children and/or grandchildren to visit you at various ports of call

- whether or not you will retain land-based telecommunications services (telephone, e-mail, fax)

- whether or not you engage a professional mail-forwarding service

- the extent to which you plan to tour and sightsee on land while cruising

- whether or not you enjoy cooking on board and the extent to which you plan to eat out

- your spending attitude when you set out

This last point is an important factor. Those who set out with a vacation mindset are likely to spend much more on sightseeing, onshore entertainment, souvenirs, and dining out. When you first set out you'll likely do much of the same: you have worked hard in the months and years leading up to your departure and you will likely want and need a vacation. For this reason, many cruisers report spending more during their first year of cruising than in subsequent years. If you set out with a mindset that this is your new lifestyle, you're more likely to replicate the day-to-day spending habits you had on land (this can be a good thing or a bad thing for your budget, depending on how disciplined you were on land!).

There are some other key factors that will affect your spending.

- **Maintenance.** Boats are like houses in that they require routine maintenance and repairs. These can be very expensive if you are paying for the labor of others. Consider, for example, the cost difference between hiring a contractor to reshingle your roof and doing it yourself. You can expect to spend up to ten times more for labor alone to hire someone to sand and paint the bottom of your boat, compared with the cost of doing it yourself.

- **Emergencies, unanticipated expenses.** Unanticipated expenses for a major rigging or engine failure, or for the loss of a dinghy due to a snapped painter or theft, can often drain your cruising kitty of a month's worth of expenses. Flights home for family-related events—such as a child's wedding, the birth of a grandchild, or a parent's illness or death— can also cut deeply into the cruising budget. Many cruisers have an emergency kitty from which they access reserves for unanticipated expenses. When these funds become depleted, they make efforts to restore the emergency reserve. This most often involves finding ways to earn an income along the way. Bartering with fellow cruisers is also a common and inexpensive way to obtain necessary services and goods.

How Do Cruisers Afford the Lifestyle?
By now I am sure you may be wondering, "If a person doesn't have to be rich, then where does the money come from?" Below is a list of the most common types of cruisers and the ways they sustain themselves, listed in their order of prevalence. They include

- those who are retired and have a guaranteed monthly income

- those who have sold a business and are living off the profits

- those who have become unemployed and been awarded a substantial severance package

- those who have accumulated savings to sustain themselves for a specific duration (e.g. teachers on a one- to two-year sabbatical)

- those who have sold everything and are living on a monthly budget and/or plan to cruise until funds are depleted

- those who have amassed some savings and plan to cruise for as long as their pocketbook enables them

- those who have downsized and are using their profits from real-estate gains to cruise for a specific period of time

- those who have portable careers and/or are continuing to earn income as they cruise

- those who cruise part time and live on land part time where they amass funds for their sojourns

- any combination of the above

This list isn't exhaustive. It merely outlines the most common ways cruisers acquire the financial wherewithal to embark on their lives afloat. While living on a retirement income tops the list, most cruisers will be the first to tell you not to wait until you have reached retirement age to pursue the cruising dream. Many are heeding this advice, as evidenced in a small but growing trend of people who are choosing to cruise in their 40s and early 50s—even though they are aware that they are forfeiting some of their best income-earning years (see sidebar, next page).

## JOAN AND JACK: HEADING TO SEA IN THEIR PRIME

Joan and Jack, both teachers in their early 50s, had just sent their third and youngest child off to university when they decided to take an unpaid, one-year sailing sabbatical. They had originally planned to retire on to a boat in their early 60s, but the sudden death of a close friend at age 49 prompted them to rethink their plans and take advantage of their excellent health and stable resources.

They refinanced their home to purchase a modest vessel and borrowed enough money to sustain themselves for 12 to 18 months. By renting their home, they were able to meet their loan payments and other land expenses while cruising. They planned to sell the boat when they returned to pay off the outstanding loan.

When they were 9 months into their sabbatical they found they were enjoying their cruising dream so much that they requested an additional one-year leave. They cruised for 23 months before returning to land and resuming their teaching positions.

A few of their friends and colleagues were aghast at Joan and Jack's decision to forgo income during their peak earning years. Jack countered these criticisms by rationalizing that he would rather spend an extra year or two in the classroom at age 60 than forgo a once-in-a-lifetime opportunity while in the best of health at age 52.

Four years after returning from their cruising sabbatical, Jack died of a massive heart attack at age 59. At Jack's memorial service, Joan described the time they spent cruising as the best two years of their lives together. She confessed that the idea of sailing off into the sunset had always appealed more to Jack. She also recalled with humor how well-meaning friends and family tried to encourage them to postpone their cruising plans until they had acquired more sailing skills and experience. In her closing remarks, Joan urged well-wishers to live their dreams today and not to be brainwashed into believing that circumstances will somehow be better in the distant future.

*Working while You Cruise*
Some cruisers plan to work along the way. You may have been told that you will have little difficulty finding work as you voyage around the world; you may also have been told that finding work is not only difficult but fraught with legalities. There is truth in both perspectives.

Finding work as you travel depends on the skills you have and whether or not the country where you want to work has a need for your talents. Skilled tradesmen such as plumbers, electricians, carpenters, and mechanics (especially diesel) continue to be in demand in many less-developed countries. Shipwrights are currently

---

### WORKING WITHOUT A WORK VISA

In most countries, it is illegal to obtain paid work unless you are a citizen or a "resident alien." As a cruiser with a tourist or cruiser's visa, whether or not you can "get away" with working illegally without a work visa depends primarily on factors beyond your control and, sometimes, beyond your ken. Countries that have traditionally been popular cruising destinations are in recent years becoming less tolerant of cruisers and other visitors who in essence take work away from the countries' citizens and legal residents.

Always bear in mind that laws regarding work and penalties regarding illegal work vary widely from place to place and even from year to year. And, even if local officials are willing to look the other way while you work under the table, local residents might not be as tolerant, and you might be subjected to unpleasant consequences apart from legal ones.

Unless you have the stomach for the possible—or likely—undesired consequences, it's best to replenish your kitty through legal avenues only and leave the risky behavior to the Around Alone competitors.

---

in great demand in many of the more developed Caribbean islands. Computer programmers and networkers are increasingly in demand, and English-language instructors rarely fall out of favor in some parts of the world. If you find yourself needing to secure work, your best bet is to talk with local cruisers about the need of the day, work laws, and the local situation.

Several women cruisers worked from their boats by providing services such as hairstyling, sewing, and sail repair. Others reported success in finding odd jobs (which usually lasted only a few days or weeks) such as housecleaning, bartending, waiting tables, house- or boat-sitting, doing brightwork, and standing in as a galley chef on charterboats. If you choose to work without the appropriate visa, be prepared to take your chances and, as they say, pay your dues, which could mean payment of heavy fines, deportation, jail, or a combination of these.

> **"It took us eighteen months to get all our papers in order, but we started work two weeks after arriving."**
> Eᴌᴀɴᴀ

The most sensible way to replenish your kitty is to obtain legal work, probably in your home country. Some couples return to their land bases for a few months each year to pick up odd jobs or do contract work they have arranged in advance. In addition to restoring the cruising kitty, this provides an opportunity to visit with family members and take care of any medical needs. Others prearrange jobs and visas in a place along their traveling route. This is what Elana, age 38, did.

*We'd always dreamed of visiting New Zealand. When we decided to sail to the South Pacific, this seemed like the perfect opportunity to spend extended time there if we could find work. I was able to obtain a [work] visa and a six-month teaching contract. My partner set something up with an engineering company. It took us eighteen months to get all our* papers in order, but we started work two weeks after arriving. We didn't earn huge amounts: the salaries are modest compared to what we made in Wisconsin. But we earned enough to top up the kitty, and the bonus was meeting so many wonderful people and having them show us parts of the island we likely wouldn't have seen.

## Money: Yours, Mine, and Ours

Jeannie and her partner had disagreements over spending decisions and money management long before they went cruising, but their different approaches to finances reached a near-crisis point when they went cruising, as Jeannie explains.

We scrimped and saved for five years to buy a boat, purchase equipment, and stash money to live on. It wasn't easy. There were times when I wanted to splurge on a new outfit and go out somewhere fancy for dinner, but [my partner] always said we couldn't afford it. Sometimes I'd pick up take-out dinner on the way back to the boat after work and [my partner] would say that I'd just prolonged our stay at the dock. We finally left in September, and I was ready for some fun! For Thanksgiving a lot of other cruisers anchored nearby, and they planned to go ashore for dinner at a little place off the beaten track. A local woman was cooking an island dinner just for them. They invited us along, but [my partner] said we couldn't afford it. That's when I put my foot down: if living on a boat meant that we couldn't even enjoy a modest meal on shore once in a while, then this wasn't the life for me!

> "If living on a boat meant that we couldn't even enjoy a modest meal on shore once in a while, then this wasn't the life for me!"
>
> JEANNIE

If you and your partner have similar disagreements on spending, work these out before you leave land. Talk about the kinds of things you envision spending money on. If he insists on keeping a firm lock on your funds, rethink your plans.

Some of the most poignant stories about cruising that have been related to me over the years concern money management—specifically his reluctance to give her access to their money when she wanted to buy something, or call home, or (this was the worst scenario I heard of) when she wanted to take the first flight home after learning at sea how truly incompatible she and her partner were.

If you and your partner regard one another as equal partners and you have a mutual respect, you may not experience friction over how you manage your funds. But if you have regular disagreements about money on land and/or your partner tends to keep a rather tight rein on the purse strings, expect both to intensify when you move on board. Your partner is probably intent on extending the cruising lifestyle as long as he can, which means he will want your money to last as long as possible.

Women whose partners are self-appointed ministers of finance offer the following words of advice.

- Establish your own cruising kitty before you set out and make this a fund only you have access to. At minimum, have enough funds in reserve for a return flight to the mainland and your associated expenses. Also factor in money for telephone calls, postcards and postage, and gifts and souvenirs for yourself and other family members.

- If you plan to keep your land-based home, and both the home and the boat are solely in your partner's name, transfer the deed on one of these assets to your name. Your preference should be the home. Knowing that you have something of value to fall back on should you discover the cruising life is not for you decreases your vulnerability. And knowing that you have some security in equity back on land may sustain you longer in the cruising lifestyle.

- You and your partner may have assets that you acquired prior to your relationship. If one or both of you plan to sell your assets in order to invest in a boat, allocate a portion of these to your personal cruising kitty and negotiate a contract before you set out. This agreement should ensure an equal division of monies invested, in the event you and your partner decide to go your separate ways.

- In addition to a cruising kitty, or as an alternative, secure a credit card in your name prior to departing and tuck it away for emergency use. In a pinch, your credit card can be used to access cash, purchase an airline ticket, and pay for accommodation and meals. Don't leave home without it!

- Have a candid, heart-to-heart discussion with your partner about each of your budgetary expectations before you sell any of your land-based assets and sail off. If you envision living on a set amount each month and the amount he envisions is considerably less, you need to discuss how each of you arrived at your calculations. For example, your budget may include eating out once a week, whereas his may include eating out once a month.

For many of the women in my study, the issue of finances did not focus on whether these women and their partners could afford to go cruising: it was more a question of what they would have to sell or forfeit to make his dream a reality.

For most men I came across, my partner included, going cruising was contingent on liquidating land-based assets. Selling out, however, was not my first choice—nor is it the only way that many couples have realized the cruising dream. The majority of cruisers I have interviewed over the years did not sell out, nor do they recommend it. The pros and cons of selling out, and some viable alternatives when individuals are ambivalent about liquidating land-based assets, are discussed in chapter 7.

## FEAR OF DISAPPOINTING A PARTNER

Many women who felt ambivalent about going cruising were not certain they would enjoy the cruising life. But their issue was not only a question of whether they'd like this new lifestyle: many were concerned that they would disappoint their partners if they did not like cruising and could not adapt to life afloat.

Travel to exotic places and freedom from the routine of land-based life may sound enticing, but in many cases there are corresponding uncertainties about living in a much smaller space, having less personal privacy, and not having the physical and psychological stamina for the lifestyle in general. Some also feared that a faltering relationship on land would list badly at sea without land distractions to give it ballast.

Remember, there is no guarantee that you (or your partner for that matter!) will love the cruising life. But if you have little or no prior boating experience, you will not know if you like the cruising lifestyle until you try it. How much should you sacrifice to make the discovery one way or the other? While there is a very good chance the lifestyle will captivate and intrigue you, there is also a chance you'll discover this lifestyle is not for you.

Erica, a 46-year-old professor at a small college, explored the idea of life on a boat with her partner but ultimately decided it held little attraction for her. She and her partner remained a couple, but Erica chose not to accompany him on a three-year circumnavigation—an adventure he had planned since his youth.

*I'm not a boat person. I love my space and my privacy, and I don't really like the water. I'm not attracted to warm climates at all: the heat bothers me and the boat does not have air conditioning. But [my partner] can't wait to get away from the rain and sleet of our winters, and he thrives in the warmth of the tropics. I'd rather explore Europe by land. European history and societies fascinate me. This summer I'm going on a paid three-month sabbatical to do research. . . . I don't want to give up my job. I'm only ten years away from a healthy pension and if I leave now, I'll never be able to retire.*

*[My partner] wants to go cruising and I am encouraging him. He has looked forward to this for too long. We plan to meet at different places as he makes his way. Maybe he'll come home once or twice a year. He plans to take on crew for the longer crossings.*

*We trust each other and believe this experience will make our relationship stronger. Yes, we will each be experiencing life in different ways and we'll share our experiences. Yes, he respects my choice and I respect his.*

After exploring the idea, some women concluded the cruising life was not for them and they chose to stay on land. But that period of exploration was not wasted. Most reported that they discovered things about themselves and their partners that ultimately enhanced the land-based lives they eventually chose.

Your partner may be disappointed with your discovery that the cruising life is not for you, but you will be more disappointed with yourself if you prematurely close the door on an opportunity to experience what most people only dream about. Share your ambivalence with your partner before you set out. Waiting until after you have quit your job and sold out will only lead to bitterness and resentment on your part, and betrayal on his part.

# 4

# What's in the Cruising Lifestyle for Me?

"The people who get on in this world are the people who get up and look for the circumstances they want, and if they can't find them, make them."

GEORGE BERNARD SHAW

WHEN MY PARTNER BEGAN TALKING ABOUT living on a boat, one of my first thoughts was, "What am I going to do on a boat?" But when I explored the idea further, my question was not simply *what* I would do on board: I wondered how I was going to bring the life I enjoyed on land onto a boat.

I loved my active land life. I prided myself on maintaining a wellness routine that included a vigorous morning workout, walking a couple of miles each day, and adhering to a Mediterranean-type diet replete with good wine and a steady supply of fresh produce. How could I replicate that kind of life on a boat?

I initially thought boaters were people who spent weekends on their pleasure vessels, partied a lot, slept late, and partied a lot (in that order); I imagined that they knitted and read a lot (if they were women) and washed, polished, and repaired their vessels a lot (if they were men); I saw them as a sedentary lot more inclined to feast on hot dogs, beer, and canned beans than a grilled chicken breast, tossed salad, and glass of wine.

My life was very different from my image of the boating life, and it prompted me to wonder what the cruising life could offer me. I did not for a moment stop to think there were things I could do on a boat that I could not do on land. That discovery came later when I stopped focusing on what I was losing by going cruising—and started focusing instead on what I could gain. I began to see that cruising offered an opportunity for self-discovery and personal renewal.

The late Hart Massey went cruising on the canals of France with his wife Melodie and their dog Joss in the 1980s, when they were in their mid-60s, on a 60-foot barge named *Lionel*. "Through this old barge we had seen France in a way we could not have done otherwise," he wrote, in closing his book *Travels with Lionel*. "It had brought us many new friends and, because of it, we had discovered a new, revitalized existence together. It was as if a new dimension had been added late in life when one wondered if any more would come along."

Cruising can expand your life and enhance the relationships you have with yourself, your partner, and those around you. You'll discover that the lifestyle contrasts sharply with the life you live on land, but the differences will refresh and inspire you. In this chapter, you learn what cruising women came to value about their lives on the water.

## EꞰTICIꞰG FACTORS

Your land-based lifestyle may be very fulfilling; but that does not preclude the possibility that what lies over the horizon can be equally as fulfilling—or even more so.

But what is it that propels someone to leave a satisfying life on land for a lifestyle that is largely an unknown? Women who have done just that revealed some of their enticing factors. These included

- the opportunity to travel extensively

- the lure of adventure, and curiosity about the unknown

- the romance of sailing off into the horizon

- the tranquility of the water

- having more time for reflection, fewer external demands, and a schedule that is almost entirely self-imposed

- the feeling that there must be more to life than simply buying and accumulating bigger, better, and newer "stuff"

- the feeling that there must be more to life in one's later years than gardening and looking after grandchildren

- the feeling that "later" may never come, that at any time health problems may prevent voyaging on a boat

- the feeling of mortality

- the desire to be different and to differentiate oneself

- the need for personal challenge

- the fear of one day regretting not having seized the moment

- an unexplainable desire to make a change

- the desire to retain one's partner

- the desire to encourage and support one's partner's growth needs

The list above includes some compelling reasons for making a lifestyle change. But for some of the women in my study, their reasons for going cruising were different: they saw going cruising as a means to another end. Peg's story is a good example.

Peg and her husband set off on their sailing vessel when they were both 65 years old. Peg's husband had sailed for many years on a variety of boats—but always with male friends. "He knew I hated boats, and after a while he stopped asking me along," said Peg. When he retired at 63, Peg's husband expressed his dream of doing some extended cruising before his health prevented him from cruising. He wanted Peg to accompany him and would not venture forth without her.

They cruised for two years, and I interviewed Peg eight years after she and her partner returned to land. Asked why she felt compelled to accompany her partner and what she gained from the experience, Peg explained.

*I hated boats, and I still hate boats. This was something that he really wanted to do. I tried to talk him into doing it with a couple of his male friends, but he was adamant that I go along or he was not going. I didn't want to live out the rest of my life knowing I had stood in the way of his dream.*

*So we sold the house and put our heirlooms in storage. I cried when I had my garage sale and people offered a pittance of what I'd paid for so many lovely things. But in the end that's all they really were: just a collection of things. The truth is, I was ready for a change. We'd lived in the same town for more than thirty years. I had done pretty well. I had been writing a social column for our local paper for a number of years, but that was getting old. I found myself thinking, "Is this all there is?" Our daughter and her sons lived more than a thousand miles away. My husband had retired two years prior, and he had no real ties in our town.*

*This boat was my ticket out. I realized that if we went cruising, we wouldn't come back to this town, so I agreed to try it out for two years and he agreed that if I wanted to return to land after two years, we would settle near our daughter.*

*Well, it was the worst two years of my life. I hated the boat, the cramped space. The weather was awful more often than not. Even my dog hated it!*

**"I** learned more about myself in those two years [on board] than in all the years before that."

P E G

*But you know, I wouldn't have traded it for anything. I learned more about myself in those two years than in all the years before that. . . . I made a lot of decisions about how I wanted to live my life when we returned to land one day, and I've stuck to those decisions.*

Peg was enticed to go cruising because she saw it as an opportunity to make a change in her life. While the cruising lifestyle was not the end she sought, it helped her to move toward a life she wanted.

What does the cruising lifestyle hold for you? What do you find enticing about the lifestyle? If you cannot think of anything, you're not trying hard enough! Perhaps the cruising life holds the potential for a future lifestyle change, as it did for Peg.

## THE POSSIBILITIES IN CRUISING

If you stopped thinking about all the reasons why you can't live on a boat and considered the reasons why you can, the many ways cruising can benefit you will begin to come clear. Resistance is a powerful force: in its absence, innumerable possibilities emerge.

Making a list of the activities you might do on a boat is a sure way to learn that you will not be bored when you set sail.

But there is a difference between making a list of potential time-fillers and focusing on activities that will fill you with a sense of productivity, fulfillment, and worth. Here are some of the ways that the cruising lifestyle benefited the women who risked making the change.

### A SIMPLER LIFE
For many cruising women, living on the water gave them a chance to live a simpler and less materialistic life—one that was not driven by consumerism.

### MORE TIME
Cruising women had more time to develop new skills and passions. Not only did they have time to learn how to handle their boats and navigate; they also had extra hours to read, write, hike, go bird-watching, take photographs, sketch, make their own clothes, paint, swim, stargaze, commune with nature, snorkel, dive, and bake bread. Beyond these activities, the pace of the cruising life gave these women more time to reflect on what they wanted out of life (as opposed to what others wanted from them).

### IMPROVED PHYSICAL HEALTH AND WELL-BEING
The day-to-day life afloat helped many women improve their health and well-being. Water sports, exploring on shore by foot, getting more fresh air, sleeping more, the natural body massage when the boat rocks gently at anchor, the exertion of hoisting sails and climbing above and below deck, hauling groceries and laundry and water in and out of dinghies, eating less junk food, and consuming less meat and more fish were some of the things that enhanced their physical health. Many women reported an improvement in their psychological health. The fol-

lowing were some of the factors that played a role: less work-related stress; less day-to-day contact with the worries of land-based family and friends; the sense of achievement from having made a major lifestyle change; increased self-awareness and self-confidence; and a chance for self-reflection and self-discovery.

## IMPROVED RELATIONSHIPS AND AWARENESS

Many women living on boats experienced a sense of renewal in their relationship with their partner. They also reported that cruising gave them an opportunity to discover (or rediscover) who they are, what they wanted out of life, and a chance to develop spiritual insight and awareness.

## DISCOVERING YOUR SELF, DISCOVERING NEW STRENGTHS

Women who made this major life change felt that the experience helped them discover new facets of themselves. Among the qualities they discovered were: inner strengths they never knew they had; a sense of adventure; a propensity for risk taking; an affinity with the water; and greater reliance on their own intuition when they were at the mercy of the elements. For Cheryl, a 39-year-old junior executive, cruising helped her to make many positive changes in her life and perceptions about herself.

> **"I'm discovering things about myself that I don't think I'd have discovered on land."**
>
> CHERYL

*I still can't believe that I am living on a boat. My friends can't believe it; the people I work with can't believe it. I'm a city gal at heart! I thought my parents would be more shocked than anybody. But when I told my mom that [my partner] and I were thinking of moving onto a boat and sailing around the world, she surprised me by saying this was the best thing that could happen to me. For a long time I wondered what she'd meant. After we'd been living aboard for three years and had done a fair bit of coastal cruising, I asked her about that comment. She said I'd never really come into my own on land; she and my dad thought cruising might bring out the best in me. They were right. I'm discovering things about myself that I don't think I'd have discovered on land—like standing on deck in the pouring rain. I complained constantly about being caught in the rain back home. And I used to curse the birds who woke me up before dawn. Now I lie awake and delight in their songs.*

## INDEPENDENCE

Many women reported a greater sense of independence. Factors that contributed to this included: liberation from the traditional workforce; fewer time constraints; less dependency on others for the provision of basic needs; increased self-confidence, often from an increase in skill and knowledge about sailing and its related systems; and much greater insight about themselves, their partner, and the world around them.

## BECOMING PART OF A COMMUNITY

One refreshing bonus of going cruising was becoming part of a unique community and enjoying the camaraderie among people who live on boats. There is a strong interdependency among cruisers. "We all need one another in a way that you don't need people on land," said Mickey, age 38.

Women who had little participation in social activities on land, beyond those they engaged in with their partner and immediate family, were struck by the highly supportive, communal aspect of cruising. Mickey offered this comparison between land life and life on a boat.

*I lived in the same apartment building for eight years and didn't socialize with a soul. You'd pass someone in the hall, but other than exchanging hellos, you didn't get involved with anyone. I can't tell you the names of any of the people who lived there. I have no idea what these people did for a living, where they worked, whether they had pets or kids. But after eight days at our marina, I knew everybody who lived aboard and we were making plans to share a pizza or a day sail. It's totally different. [In this lifestyle] you have so much in common with people who are enjoying many of the same things you are.*

*People who live on boats are always willing to lend a helping hand. Last week [my partner] was wrestling with a repair job and the guy across the slip yelled over, "I'll be right over," and he came over and knew exactly what to do. I remember struggling to change a tire in the parking lot at our apartment; at least six people walked by me and not one offered to help.*

Many attribute the interdependency among cruisers to the heightened vulnerability to the elements. Day-to-day life revolves around the weather. Voyages will be shortened, extended, or postponed depending on weather fronts. Shifting winds in the middle of the night may prompt your immediate evacuation from an anchorage that has been a safe, sheltered haven for three weeks. There is a constant dialogue among cruisers about what the weather holds, and about what you hear on different radio broadcasts throughout the day. The very nature of the lifestyle encourages interdependency and camaraderie.

## Being Seen as a Person Apart from Careers or Past Roles

Another refreshing difference between landlubbers and cruisers is that the majority of cruisers do not define themselves by their professions or their education. Everyone is a sailor, a cruiser, or a liveaboard: whatever you were in your previous life is of little importance.

## OTHER DISCOVERIES

Cruising women, myself included, made other kinds of discoveries at sea. These may not have been life-altering revelations, but they were still important lessons learned. We found

- that we can prepare gourmet extravaganzas without 14 spatulas, 16 mixing bowls, and 13 electrical appliances

- that fish talk

- that my partner and I can thrive in a very small space

- that we need not feel guilty about spending the entire morning photographing flowers or cavorting with the fish on a reef

- that the classics we despised in high school make for a terrific read

- that maybe Henry Thoreau was really onto something at Walden Pond

- that fine wine can be had and stored at sea as well as on land

- that we can draw, paint, and even sell our masterpieces

- that sunrises are as magnificent as sunsets

- that solitude can be reenergizing

- that the ocean is not always a raging swirl of wind and water and can be like a mill pond for 10 days or more

- that there will be days when I actually pray for wind

- that dolphins smile

- that people the world over are generally kind and good

- that I crave adventure and exploring the unknown no less than my partner

- that I am more of a risk taker than I previously believed

---

One woman in my study recalled the discomfort she felt every time she had to socialize with her partner's work colleagues. "I felt a sense of inadequacy whenever [my partner] and I entertained his clients," she said. "I never worked outside the home, but I sure worked in it! Out here, no one cares how much or how little education I have. Working women wouldn't give me the time of day back [on land]. But here I am an equal. People are interested in what I have to say."

The cruising lifestyle has changed my attitude and that of my partner toward our careers. Whether living on land or on the boat, we are learning to work to live rather than live to work!

### SEEING HOW YOUR LIFE IMPACTS THOSE AROUND YOU

When we take stock of our lives and enact changes, we can inadvertently prompt those closest to us to do the same. The lifestyle changes cruising women made sometimes gave family and friends the impetus to change; at the least, their cruising adventures prompted family and friends to travel to faraway places they may never have visited on their own.

Sometimes those around us choose to react in a different way; instead of celebrating and sharing in our new lifestyle, they move to safeguard all they have come to know. This has sometimes resulted in friends and family putting some space between themselves and us, so as not to disrupt the safe and contented lives they have established on land. Risk taking, after all, can be very contagious!

# LIFE IS NEVER THE SAME

Whether you go cruising for six months, a few years, or indefinitely, you will discover aspects of yourself, your partner, and your relationship that will forever change your life.

You and your partner will discover things about each other that may be pleasantly surprising and refreshing; you may also discover things that are maddening and confusing. As you cruise, you may find fulfillment where you least expect it; you may also find yourself unnerved when things that were once gratifying begin to leave you unsatisfied and empty.

The sea can bring you face-to-face with who you really are and who you have the potential to be. This can be reassuring and affirming, or it can force you to take a hard look at yourself and those closest to you—and you may find yourself having to make choices you were able to avoid making on land. These might include the following:

- that the career that consumed you on land and fed your self-esteem no longer holds much appeal for you

- that you like living in a smaller space and especially like having much less space to clean and organize on a day-to-day basis

- that you are a much better sailor than your partner and he resents this fact

- that your partner has a Jekyll-and-Hyde personality, the Jekyll side of which you did not see until after you'd cast the lines off

- that your partner hates living on a boat and that you adore it

- that you feel liberated by the cruising lifestyle but your partner now feels strangely constrained by it

- that you want to extend your sabbatical and your partner wants to shorten his

- that you will be returning to land without your partner

- that your partner will be returning to land without you

Discoveries about ourselves and our partners, while sometimes painful and threatening, provide mutual opportunities for growth and renewal. If you and your partner are committed to supporting each other's growth, then you'll find that the cruising lifestyle will be a rich and rewarding life for both of you, and the answer to your question, "what's in it for me?" will be amply rewarding.

# 5

# Managing Fear

"Don't be afraid your life will end;
be afraid that it will never begin."

GRACE HANSEN

FEAR CAN COMPEL YOU TO MAKE CHOICES.
When my partner expressed his desire to go cruising, my fear
of the water and all my related fears—of sharks, rogue waves,
and Force 10 storms, just to name a few—made cruising seem
like a very frightening undertaking. But the thought of missing
out on all the cruising life potentially held scared me more. I
came to realize that in fearing death I was also fearing life. That
fact embarrassed me and was in direct contradiction to my live-
life-to-the-fullest nature. My fear of missing out on the cruising
experience was stronger than my fear of the water—and so I
made the choice to become a cruiser.

Many women who cruise consider water a life-threatening
force. They may be afraid of it because they don't know how
to swim, or because they fear the sharks and the other underwater predators they imagine swimming below the surface. They may be afraid of setting out to cross an ocean, for
fear of encountering bad weather, being rolled by a rogue
wave, or hitting floating debris that may hole their vessel and
sink it.

Harrowing tales have appeared in the press about people who have suffered such mishaps; but remember that these incidents garnered such media attention largely because they are uncommon occurrences! Regardless of the likelihood of encountering similar disasters, the fears these cruising women identified felt very real to them.

Fear can immobilize you, and it can bring your life to a standstill if you allow it. Or, you can take control of your fears and use them to motivate you to become more knowledgeable, more skilled, and ultimately richer in experience.

Women who cruise did not let their fears stop them from moving toward a life on the water. In this chapter, you will read how other women dealt with the fears that haunted them when they considered setting out to sea.

## IDENTIFYING YOUR FEARS

The first step in managing and conquering your fears is to identify them.

I have not always understood where my fears came from. More often than not, I wrongly attributed them to surface factors, to the first thing that came to mind. I have shared that I'm afraid of the water; I'm anxious about heeling more than 20 degrees, scared of sharks, and terrified of encountering a rogue wave. In truth, water does not scare me. It soothes and revitalizes me; heeling and sitting on the windward rail on a breezy day is an exhilarating experience that cleanses my thoughts and leaves me with little more to think about than the wind on my face. Sharks fascinate me, as long as there is enough distance between me and them. And who isn't afraid of encountering a destructive rogue wave? It's not the water that scares me; rather, it's dying as a consequence of encountering a shark, or a rogue wave, or being tossed into the water while heeling and then drowning. Those are the roots of my fears.

Make a list of your fears. Write them down as quickly as they come to mind; don't spend a lot of time analyzing them at this point. This list can include fears about anything, not just what you fear about cruising.

Over time, my list has included: a fear of losing my land-based lifestyle; a fear of walking in the dark; a fear of one of my parents dying before I tell them how much they have meant to me; a fear of colliding with a partially submerged container while voyaging at night; a fear of gaining weight if I don't exercise each day; and a fear of our dog falling overboard or becoming lost in a foreign country.

Now take your list and start at the top. For each fear, ask yourself what it is about the element you've named that makes you afraid. Once you are able to identify what makes you afraid, move to a deeper level. What is it about *that* that you fear? For example, I am afraid to walk alone in the dark. Why? Because it scares me. What is it about that act that scares me? There may be someone lurking in the shadows who may harm me. It is not walking alone after dark that I fear: it's being attacked by a stranger in the shadows.

Take each of your fears through this process and see what emerges. You may find that what you thought you feared is not really what you fear at all. Once you identify your fears, you need to decide how you can conquer that fear or manage it so it does not paralyze you. The next section includes some techniques for managing fear.

## TECHNIQUES FOR MANAGING FEAR

Here are some techniques you can use in your effort to manage your fears.

## DEMYSTIFY WHAT YOU'RE AFRAID OF

One technique for overcoming fear is to demystify what it is that's making you afraid. For example, some people have made it their life's work to study the behavior of sharks. They seek out shark-infested waters and immerse themselves in the sharks' environment to gain an understanding of their habitat and their behaviors. The individuals who study sharks do not have a vague, overriding fear of these creatures: they understand them, they know what triggers their aggressive behaviors, and they know how to deal safely with them.

## GAIN MORE EXPERIENCE AND UNDERSTANDING

Gaining more experience and a better understanding of what you fear can help you manage that fear so it does not impinge on your life. My fear of heeling is a prime example.

I have not overcome my fear of heeling, but I have learned how to manage it through experience and by gaining more knowledge about how sailboats are engineered so they do not flip upside down when they heel. The more I sail on our boat, the better I understand how it works and the more I trust it.

This may sound very simple and logical, but it is very much a double-edged sword: unless I risk spending time on my boat and experiencing her at various degrees of heel, I won't be able to manage my fear. I have to risk coming face-to-face with my fear in order to learn how best to deal with it.

Several women I interviewed described how their comfort levels grew as they became more familiar with their vessels and gained more experience and confidence. One woman recalled how her fears about wind and waves were permanently assuaged when she took the helm of her boat in gale-force winds: she experienced, for the first time, a sense of exhilaration that was incomparable to anything she had experienced before.

As their self-confidence increased, most women reported that their initial fears and concerns decreased. This was especially the case with respect to their fears about the integrity of the vessel and concerns for personal safety.

Knowledge and experience are strong tools for managing or conquering fear. Books and periodicals were identified by many women as their path for managing specific fears (as well as providing valuable information about the cruising lifestyle). These resources were also the source of inspiration for many who thought, "If she can do it, then so can I!" A list of books that were most often referenced by the women I interviewed is contained in the bibliography.

### TALK YOURSELF THROUGH IT

Talking yourself through your fears is another technique for managing them. This literally means that you talk out loud to yourself about a specific fear in order to put it into perspective and neutralize it.

One day when we were sailing in gale-force winds, I sat on the windward rail and repeatedly said to myself, "This boat is built for gusty North Sea conditions; she won't fail us!" I repeated this to myself for 15 minutes and eventually settled into a comfort zone where my fear was neutralized. The fear was still there, but I was able to hold it in check without causing myself undue anxiety.

### CHANGE YOUR PERSPECTIVE

Reframing is a common technique that enables you to change your perspective from a negative to a positive. For example, a situation that is dangerous or unsafe can also be exciting and adventurous. Try reframing your fears about cruising and look at how you can alter your perspective from the negative to the positive.

Remember the woman mentioned above who took the helm in gale-force winds? She learned that handling a boat in these conditions can be exhilarating.

## What Is the Worst-Case Scenario?

Imagining the worst-case scenario is another common technique for putting fear into perspective. When fear strikes I ask myself, "What's the worst that could happen?" Then I consider my options. This technique is very similar to self-talk. In both techniques, you walk yourself through a logical process of identifying, exploring, and neutralizing the subject of your fear.

Sometimes fear can be managed simply and with practical remedies. Terry shared this example.

> **"One of my biggest fears was that I would fall asleep on watch and we'd be hit by a freighter. It turns out I'm not the only one with this fear."**
> Terry

*One of my biggest fears was that I would fall asleep on watch and we'd be hit by a freighter. It turns out I'm not the only one with this fear. I happened to share this with a group of women at one of the anchorages we spent several weeks in. One woman said she kept an egg timer in the cockpit and wound it at ten-minute intervals. I now do the same thing. It's amazing that such a little gadget could have such an effect.*

And sometimes managing one's fear is more complex. Brenda's story illustrates this.

*I was in therapy for the last two years we lived on land before moving onto the boat. I was so afraid that I'd lose myself and somehow become a lesser person if I gave up my career and home and went cruising.*

*I had been groomed for success. My parents made tremendous sacrifices for my education and here I was thinking of wasting it to live on a* boat. I was afraid of disappointing them and equally afraid of disappointing or even losing [my partner]. While in therapy I learned to confront many issues that had been outstanding between me and my parents since my youth. I also learned how to assert my needs with [my partner]. This wasn't easy for me. Eventually he voluntarily came to therapy with me because I couldn't bring myself to do some of the things the therapist was suggesting. I think in some respects it also helped him sort out some issues, like his fear of living too long in one place and his own fear of success.

> "**There was a part of me that really wanted to go cruising. I saw it as a way to break free from my parents. I also saw it as a way to do something different.**"
>
> BRENDA

The funny thing is there was a part of me that really wanted to go cruising. I saw it as a way to break free from my parents. I also saw it as a way to do something different. I'd chosen my career based on what my parents thought was best for me and the truth is I was never passionate about it. But I was so afraid of telling anyone how I felt—I didn't even tell [my partner] until we were in therapy together.

The therapist helped me sort out a lot of things. In a way she gave me permission to make choices that I wanted to make for me. I chose to try out life on a boat and you know, I love it!

## WHEN YOUR PARTNER DOESN'T SHARE YOUR FEAR

One of the factors that makes managing fear such a daunting task is that our fears are uniquely ours, and they typically don't have as powerful an impact on those around us. But if you don't learn to manage them, your fears can flow over into your relationship with your partner.

Trying to convey the intensity of your fears to someone who does not possess a similar fear can be very frustrating. And the longer your fear haunts you, the greater your sense of failure is for having failed to overcome something that is a nonevent for the person you love most. Lorna, age 35, had a partner who did not understand the depth of fear she experienced during an overnight passage. This is her story.

*I was on watch one night and [my partner] was asleep below. It was so dark, not a star in sight—and my night vision is poor to begin with. I was always afraid of hitting something in the water that I wouldn't be able to see with enough time to avoid it. This night I had an uneasy feeling. I couldn't put it into words, so I didn't even tell [my partner]. Around 3 A.M. I caught a glimpse of something just barely sticking up in the water. To this day I still don't know how I saw it. I turned the helm too sharply, which caused the sails to flail about and this woke [my partner]. He came on deck. For several minutes, he didn't know what had happened and I couldn't stop shaking and crying long enough to tell him. I was paralyzed with fear—of what might have happened if I'd hit that object.*

*He tried to calm me down and eventually I was able to tell him that we almost collided with something. Later we decided it must have been a submerged container. He asked me why I was shaking and why I was crying so hard. After all, I hadn't hit anything and we were doing fine. He couldn't relate to my fear. If he'd been at the helm and I'd been asleep below, he would have steered off course to avoid the collision, but it wouldn't have been a big deal to him. He probably wouldn't have mentioned it until sometime the next day. This really bothered me, that he was so unable to relate to my fear. I thought about his reaction long afterward. It wasn't that he was critical of what I had done: he praised my actions, and he didn't ridicule my crying or shaking. He just couldn't relate to it.*

My fear of the water and of heeling surprised my partner. "I had no idea how terrified you were of these things," he told me. He was seeing this aspect of me for the first time, and revealing these fears was to me an admission of failure. But I felt I had let my partner down, because he knew me on land to be a fairly fearless individual. On land I was in control of my environment and in familiar territory; at sea I felt out of control and at the mercy of the elements. I was also initially intimidated by sailing, an activity I knew next to nothing about.

At one point my partner questioned whether he could, in good conscience, ask me to continue in a lifestyle that had elements that terrified me. He shared his concerns one night, before we decommissioned our boat and hauled her out for the hurricane season. If I wanted to sell the boat and land-cruise instead, he would acquiesce to this without bitterness.

I was deeply moved, both by his concern and by the fact that he would give up a lifestyle he loved to accommodate my fears. I decided then that I had to find a way to manage my fears for both of us: for me, because I didn't like living with such terror; for my partner, because I knew how much the cruising dream meant to him. My fears stopped being just my own: they grew to the point where they affected someone else's life, perhaps even more than they affected me.

My fears did not dissipate overnight, but in time I became a less anxious, more confident, and more enthusiastic sailor. Taking the helm more often helped me develop a sense of control over our vessel and let me decide how tight I wanted to sail to the wind (the tighter a vessel sails, the more she heels). There were even times when my partner wanted to reduce sail before I did in order to reduce our degree of heel! Maneuvering our vessel more often during docking and anchoring procedures has helped me to develop confidence in my ability to handle our vessel in tight conditions.

But the biggest change has been in my attitude and specifically my determination to keep the bigger picture in mind.

After all, the amount of time most cruisers actually spend sailing is tiny compared to the amount of time they spend at anchor and exploring both above the sea and beneath it.

Much of what we fear is fear itself—as though fear has a face and taunts us whenever we dare to venture off a worn and familiar path. There is no shortage of people, places, and things to fear. But if you let your fears overcome you, you will curl up and die a slow death out of boredom and despair. Sadly, I know people (and I trust you do too) who will never see much of the world because they are afraid of flying; there are people who consider New York far too dangerous to visit; there are those who would never risk a moonlit walk down the shore of a deserted tropical island. Every choice you make is fraught with hazards. But the extent to which you let those restrict you from taking risks, from making changes, and from growing is very much in your control.

Many women embarked on the cruising lifestyle with minimal sailing experience, and they naturally harbored fears about this new life—from heeling, to encountering bad weather, to having their partners fall overboard, to being shipwrecked at sea. But the majority of these women reported that most of their fears dissipated over time as they gained experience and an increase in self-confidence.

It takes inner strength to confront your fears, but you can take control of them and stop them from controlling you.

# 6

# The Cruising Couple: Interpersonal Dynamics

"Do unto others as others would have you do
unto them."

HARVILLE HENDRIX

WHEN WAS THE LAST TIME YOU AND YOUR
partner stole a weekend away together, free from the distractions of children, relatives, friends, and colleagues? What sorts
of things did you do together? Did you laugh together and delight in each other's company? Did either of you indulge in a
solitary activity—a quiet walk at dawn, or an hour with a good
book? Were you supportive of each other's need for solitude?
What did you talk about over dinner? Were you at a loss for
words? Did you feel that your partner listened to what you had
to say, and were you an attentive audience in return? As the
weekend drew to a close, did you wish you had another day or
two together? Or did you breathe a sigh of relief?

The answers to these questions may reveal more to you about
your relationship than you realize. If you and your partner enjoy
each other's company and look forward to time together free of
day-to-day distractions, then you are likely to enjoy the cruising
life. But if your relationship has shades of Vicky and Nick's, described below, then you may not be well-suited to the cruising life.

Vicky and Nick, who are five years into their retirement,

appear to be an active, happy couple whose days are jammed from dawn to dusk. They spend their days hiking, bicycling, canoeing, camping, skiing, or participating in a variety of community events. On most evenings, they have guests for dinner or they dine out. So what's wrong with this picture?

In their more than thirty years of marriage they have not spent as much as a weekend by themselves, and they have never vacationed without the company of friends or family. Where their children once accompanied them around the globe—the last of whom left home eight years ago—friends now stand in.

On the outside they appear to enjoy a happy, solid relationship; but after a few hours in their company, one finds the cracks in their veneer to be painfully obvious. Vicky cannot complete a sentence without being interrupted by Nick, who clarifies the points she tries to make, corrects trivial details of her story, challenges her if he disagrees, and eventually takes over the discussion while she remains silent. It is not the continual interrupting that is disconcerting; it's his tone of voice and the way he challenges, disagrees, and ridicules his partner. I cannot recall a time when Nick has behaved otherwise.

Many relationships that endure on land will not survive the cruising lifestyle. Is there something about the cruising lifestyle that spells doom for couples who are already in distress, knowingly or not? That answer is yes, and no.

Land life offers many distractions that can enable the worst of relationships to endure until "death do them part." The day-to-day demands of children, grandchildren, careers, elderly parents, friends, extended family, social obligations, and community responsibilities leave little time to resolve interpersonal issues. Couples who have been too distracted to address their issues on land may find they are strangers at sea—or that they don't even like each other!

Relationships that suffer from the demands of land life, however, are not hopeless when it comes to going cruising. Gail, age 52, and her partner are just one example. They enjoyed a strong bond as a couple in their early years together, but they eventually grew apart to become virtual strangers. Still, their fondness for each other endured, as well as their mutual respect. The cruising life gave them the time and opportunity to rekindle their relationship. This is Gail's story.

*We were so busy in the months before we left to go cruising. Two of our daughters were married, and our first grandchild came along. [My partner's] mother was in and out of the hospital. I was trying to get the house ready to sell; I had to sort through everything, trying to decide what to keep, and he was preoccupied with getting the boat ready.*

*We had friends join us for the sail down the coast, and they stayed three weeks. Three days after they left [my partner] and I were sitting on the aft deck having coffee. I found myself searching for something to say to him. The silence was awkward. It dawned on me that I could not remember the last time we had been alone together: it was like being with a stranger.*

> **"I** thought, 'I married this guy a long time ago and we used to have a lot of fun together, so maybe we can again.' And we did. It didn't happen overnight. We had a lot of catching up to do, but I'm just glad I didn't give up on us and stay on land."
>
> GAIL

*We'd had some pretty rocky times [on land]. He traveled a lot with his work. I stayed home to raise the kids and got involved in all kinds of stuff with them. I went back to work when the kids were in high school and things seemed to get crazier. All of us were coming and going at different times.*

*I didn't want to go cruising. I was finally gaining a sense of independence with the kids on their own, and I was really enjoying my work. But I gave in. It would have been real easy for me to say, "You know, I really don't want to do this. We don't even know each other any more!"*

## Is Your Relationship Strong Enough to Take to Sea?

There are no guarantees that even the best of relationships on land will endure a major lifestyle change. But there are factors that will affect the direction of the pendulum. How can you determine whether your relationship is strong enough to take to sea? The following questions raise some vital points that can make or break most cruising relationships. Take a few moments and consider this list.

1.  Do you trust your partner's judgment in most matters and does he trust yours?

2.  If you were to fall off the boat, would you trust him to rescue you? Would you make every effort to rescue him?

3.  Do you consider yourself an equal partner in your relationship? Would your partner describe you similarly?

4.  Does your partner encourage and support your efforts to learn new skills and explore new talents?

5.  Is he your fan club? Are you his?

6.  Are you able to reveal your thoughts, fears, hopes, and dreams to your partner without the fear of his ridiculing you?

7.  Do you consider your partner your best friend?

8.  Do you and your partner enjoy spending time alone together without the company of others?

If you answered *yes* to all of the above you are setting out on the right foot.

*But I thought, "I married this guy a long time ago and we used to have a lot of fun together, so maybe we can again." And we did. It didn't happen overnight. We had a lot of catching up to do, but I'm just glad I didn't give up on us and stay on land.*

## TRUST

Trust is an important element in a cruising relationship. When trust is high, we are confident and comfortable in taking risks, in stretching ourselves to learn, explore, discover. But when trust is low, we are constantly on the defensive, intent on protecting who we are and what we've got. When you sail off with your partner, you are putting your life into his hands, and he is putting his into yours. You will have to trust each other to safeguard your personal safety and your happiness.

**When you sail off with your partner, you are putting your life into his hands, and he is putting his into yours. You will have to trust each other to safeguard your personal safety and your happiness.**

Women who participated in my study vowed that they could not go to sea with a man they didn't trust. Most of them referenced the concept of entrusting their physical safety. "If I didn't trust him, I wouldn't feel safe—and if I didn't feel safe, I could not leave the dock," said one woman.

Madeline, age 60, and her partner are a poignant example of the strength that develops in a relationship where two people entrust their lives and happiness to each other.

*I know that [he] would never pursue his own dreams at my expense. He cares about my happiness and would not intentionally do something that might jeopardize my happiness. I trust him with my life.*

*One night we were talking about our cruising plans. We hadn't bought the boat at this point, and although we'd been looking, I hadn't seen anything that felt right. He said, "Maddy, the most important thing is that you like the boat, so we'll keep looking until you see one you like." I said, "I know so little about boats, about sailing. I don't know if I can do this. There's so much to learn." He turned my face toward his and said, "If you think this is too much for you, we won't do it. We'll do something else that you are more comfortable with. But I know you can do this. I know you don't think you can, but I know you: when you set your mind on learning something and doing something, you do it."*

*That was a turning point for me. I'd always known he believed in me. He wasn't trying to coerce me into anything. When he said we'd do something else if it would make me more comfortable, he didn't say this with anger or regret in his voice. He meant it. I was so moved by this. I decided then and there that if he would do that for me, then I wanted to do this for him.*

When trust is high in a relationship, partners work together on each other's behalf and share a sense of synergy that can sustain them through the best and worst times. But when trust is low, each partner closes down and stops being receptive to the other's needs.

## ROLES, EQUALITY, AND PARTNERSHIPS

Throughout this book, I use the term *partner*. I use that term deliberately and with conviction. If you are truly an equal partner in all aspects of the lifestyle change you are contemplating, then the joy and benefits you'll derive from this new life will be tremendous. But if you do not feel you are an equal player, and your partner does not treat you that way, overall satisfaction will be low for both of you.

What exactly is a partnership and what makes it equal? I define this as a state of being where both partners feel, "We are in this together, for better or worse." We often think of equal partnerships as ones where both partners contribute equal amounts of the same things. But every person has unique strengths and skills. In relationships, equality cannot be equated with how much each partner contributes in a quantitative sense. It is the quality of what we each bring to the partnership, rather than how much, that creates a powerful whole.

Take a few minutes to consider the nature of the partnership you have in your day-to-day life on land. Are you equal partners, and if so, in what respects? How do you handle finances? Do you both have equal access to bank accounts? If you do not work outside the home, does your partner perceive what you do at home to be as important as what he does in the workplace? How do you divide chores? Do you both plan social activities? Most importantly, are you both happy with the roles you have assumed?

When you start assigning a quantitative value to what each of you contributes to your relationship, then at least one of you will have to keep count. It is not strictly how you divide your day-to-day tasks but the degree of respect and value you attribute to each other's contributions. The key issue is whether the type of partnership you have forged works for you.

Now that you have a clearer view of your partnership on land, remember that your life will change when you go to sea. That is what happened to Barb and John, a couple in their mid-40s who embarked upon the cruising lifestyle two years ago.

On land, both partners worked outside the home and divided domestic tasks according to a flexible schedule. One week Barb was responsible for grocery shopping and cooking; the following week Bob assumed those responsibilities. Housecleaning was a joint venture assigned to Saturdays when they were both home to participate. Bob was responsible for buying birthday, Christmas, and other gifts for his side of the family and Barb looked after her side. When Barb and John decided to buy and refurbish a sailboat for long-term cruising, they worked side by side on most aspects of the project. Barb was not keen on learning diesel-engine maintenance, but she enjoyed maintaining the brightwork.

Once they began cruising, Barb assumed responsibility for what she calls the "pink-collar" jobs—those tasks traditionally performed by females, including provisioning, laundry, meal planning and preparation, and routine housework. Bob assumed responsibility for the "blue-collar" jobs—including engine maintenance, routine repairs to the electrical, plumbing and rigging systems, etc. Barb was initially distressed about the traditional roles they reverted to on the boat, for they had worked hard to avoid this on land.

Barb grew to realize, however, that she did not want to do the chores Bob did, and as traditional as their division of labor became, it worked for them. "The reality is, I'm good in the galley and Bob's at his best in the engine room," said Barb. "I need him there [in the engine room] as much as he needs me in the galley."

Don't assume that the nature of your partnership on land will automatically work at sea, for you may find that your respective skills will cause you to modify the roles you had. Cruising life is different than land life. You can no longer leave your car with the mechanic or call a plumber when the kitchen sink becomes clogged. Unless you have deep pockets or a hired crew, you and your partner will undertake most chores that need attention in your day-to-day cruising lives.

## MUTUAL RESPECT, POSITIVE REGARD

The mutual respect and positive regard you and your partner have for one another will sustain you through the trials and tribulations of making a lifestyle change. In the absence of these timeless ingredients, you will quickly become discouraged in your effort to adopt the cruising lifestyle. Here are some examples of the kind of mutual respect and positive regard I am referring to.

- The degree of genuine care and consideration each of you pays to the needs of the other. For example, your partner might say, "You give the word and we'll reduce sail."

- The extent to which your partner encourages and praises your efforts and, in turn, the extent to which you praise his. For example, he'll comment on a job well done when you take your boat into the slip.

- The pride that is evident in your partner's remarks when he is describing your achievements to others. For example, he may tell others, "She came through the storm with flying colors!"

- The extent to which each of you conveys your mutual value and worth. For example, telling your partner, "I couldn't do this without you."

## COMMUNICATION

When I asked women to name specific books that proved particularly helpful as they prepared for the cruising life, I expected to hear references to cruising classics written by veteran voyagers such as the Pardeys or the Hiscocks. Books by those adventurers and others were cited, but one book was referenced more often than all others combined: John Gray's book on male-female relationships, *Men Are from Mars, Women Are from Venus*.

Gray's excellent book explores how communication styles differ between men and women, and he offers practical advice on how to remedy those differences. What is surprising is the extent to which each gender assumes that the other gender understands exactly the messages they intend to convey. That situation certainly arises on boats. When one person says, "Over there!" and the other erroneously assumes "over there" to be somewhere other than where that person intended, tempers can flare—in seconds! Both partners need to take a moment and ask themselves, "What does he or she mean?" If the answer is vague, ask for clarification. On our boat, "over there" has been replaced with the positions on a clock. "Steer to three o'clock" is more precise and less likely to create confusion. Unfortunately, most communication problems cannot be solved with clock analogies.

The ways we communicate become so habitual over time that we are often unaware when communication with our partners becomes somehow dysfunctional. But when circumstances in our lives change, habits no longer work as well as they used to. It is interesting to note that most women sought advice from Gray's book after they had set sail and experienced a change in their circumstances.

You may wonder how this could be. Didn't they have communication problems on land? Again, yes and no. Remember those day-to-day distractions I referred to earlier? In the midst of our chaotic lives on land, we are often too tired to review the day's events with our partners. Maybe a close friend, a sister, or your mother was more accessible, or maybe you were more comfortable discussing matters with someone other than your partner. You may also have avoided talking with your partner about issues that caused stress and conflict.

No one person can be expected to meet all of our needs: life on land gives us access to many individuals with whom we forge meaningful relationships. Your partner is likely one of several people who satisfy your emotional and intellectual needs. But at sea, when those other people are no longer accessible on a day-to-day basis, you will naturally turn to the one person who is: your partner.

If you enjoy open, honest communication with your partner on land, you will almost certainly enjoy the same at sea. But if you are experiencing communication difficulties before you set sail, then they will likely continue once you go cruising.

Women who did not share a communicative relationship with their partners on land were sometimes surprised to discover that this pattern continued after they went cruising. Equally surprising was the realization that since he had not been expected to meet all her needs on land, he almost certainly did not expect to have to do so at sea. Her disappointment in his failure to live up to her expectations as a listener and a confidant often caused the classic lament, "You don't understand me!" and was met with the classic retort, "I don't know what you want!"

A new lifestyle brings many changes, both positive and negative, to how partners interact and communicate. Changes in your respective roles, routines, and expectations can transform your existing relationship—to one from which you derive greater joy and fulfillment. Being able to communicate your wants and needs openly, honestly, and in a way that is nonjudgmental and free of criticism will be an ongoing challenge once you set sail. But if you manage to succeed, it's a challenge that will be well worth the effort.

## YELLING

Few experiences are as degrading and humiliating as being yelled at, yet this is the most frequently reported source of stress among cruising couples. Being yelled at is often the only major complaint women have about their partners. But in a few instances, the yelling was so severe that the women chose to jump ship to avoid being continually berated by their partner.

Ironically, the majority of men who yell don't intend to hurt or humiliate their partners, and they don't perceive their behavior as abusive. They see yelling as a way of conveying a sense of urgency when they need something done quickly and immediately. But there is yelling and there is *yelling*! For most women, it's not the yelling by itself that is disconcerting: it's the way in which it is done.

Yelling that has undertones of sarcasm and criticism—and implies the person on the receiving end is inadequate—is abusive. If your partner is an abusive yeller, you need to talk to him about the effect his behavior has on you; then you need to agree on an alternate form of communication.

Some couples have learned to communicate during boat-handling maneuvers by using hand signals. This is especially helpful when you are anchoring, which is one of the most stressful tasks cruising couples do on a routine basis. Others have devised a system where the woman alerts her partner to his behavior by raising her arm—as if to say "stop"—and averting her eyes until he can convey his message in a less intimidating manner. Other couples remind each other after an incident that their positive feelings for one another prevail, even when one of them is yelling. Patricia, age 64, witnessed a fascinating dialogue between an elderly couple who were having difficulties anchoring in New York Harbor late one afternoon. Here is what she saw.

*They were trying to anchor in New York Harbor amidst commercial vessels of every sort. At any moment I was certain they were going to be run over. She was at the helm, and he was on the bow tending to the anchor. All of a sudden I heard her say in a calm, even voice, "Darling, the painter has become tangled in the prop." Now I know what my partner would've said to me—and it was nothing like what that fellow said to his wife. In a voice as calm as hers he responded with not a hint of anger or frustration, "No need to fret my love, I'll dive on it."*

> **"When we do yell, it's often with endearments. It makes all the difference in the world to know it's the situation that has him riled, not you."**
>
> Pᴀᴛʀɪᴄɪᴀ

*He proceeded to dive on the prop and all the while she cooed words of encouragement and affection to him. "Do be careful my sweet. Let's get you into the shower quickly, shall we my love?" [My partner] and I looked at each other with genuine awe. It was as if we were hearing a foreign language.*

*A few days later [my partner] and I were setting our anchor and he looked back at me from the bow and said in one of the calmest tones I'd ever heard, "Darling, give it a little reverse, will you?" to which I replied, "Anything you say, my love." We were bent with laughter as we did this, but you know, we both yell a lot less now. And when we do yell, it's often with endearments, just as this couple did. It makes all the difference in the world to know it's the situation that has him riled, not you.*

While it's objectionable behavior in all but the most urgent circumstances, yelling is bound to occur during times of extreme stress or when you and your partner are fatigued from a long passage and emotions are raw. Once you are safely anchored or settled on a more comfortable tack, it is important that you take time to debrief and reflect on the circumstances that precipitated the outburst. Through this process, you will learn to approach similar situations differently in the future. Minimally, debriefing provides an opportunity for you to reassure each other that it was the situation that caused the outburst and not your feelings for the other person.

# TIME OUT IN A SMALL SPACE

Most couples, even those who enjoy a strong relationship, occasionally need time out from each other. Time out gives you a chance to gather your thoughts or simply reenergize; space apart is sometimes necessary too for clearing the air and diffusing tension after a stressful experience. On land, you can find physical separation in the garden, in another room, or by taking a drive in your car or going on a good long walk. Finding time out on a boat requires creativity and mutual regard for each other's need for physical and psychological space.

Some couples identify time-out areas of their boat well in advance of any need to retreat; others agree they will use a specific signal to indicate their need for solitude. Friends of ours had a unique agreement: when either one of them was wearing a specific blue cap, they were not to be disturbed (unless an emergency arose). Another woman I know claimed a certain area of her boat where she could meditate without interruption. Still another reserved the extra cabin for her downtime; she retreated here to write, draw, read, or simply to count to ten when she felt upset. Regardless of the size of your boat, every vessel has a bow and a stern; these can easily become places for retreat when your need for solitude beckons.

If you already own your vessel, take some time to consider where your time-out area might be. It is possible to achieve psychological space, even on the smallest vessels. If you are searching for your vessel, think about such a space when you look at different boats.

In North America, people have become accustomed to bigger houses that, at times, seem to swallow us up. Life on a boat can be a time when you rediscover a physical and emotional intimacy that you and your partner may have lost on land, as well as a time when you also find enough space to grow.

# Conflict

Conflict is as natural in relationships as love, passion, and jealousy. It's bound to arise in the many discussions you and your partner have as you prepare to go cruising, and it will appear again after you set sail. The areas of conflict most frequently reported by cruising couples include

- whether or not to sell out on land

- your readiness to toss the lines and set sail

- what to bring on the boat

- money management

- anchoring (because this is when most yelling occurs!)

- how long to wait for weather

- length of time in ports of call

- potential destinations

- safety considerations

- whether or not to take on crew

- boat fatigue

Many people expend tremendous amounts of energy trying to avoid conflict. In some instances, they equate conflict with physical or emotional harm. But conflict is nothing more than a difference in your opinions and feelings. Through the expression of these differences—in a calm and articulate manner—you can learn more about one another and grow as individuals and as a couple.

If conflict frightens or intimidates you, give yourself and your partner permission to disagree in constructive, nonaccusatory ways. Establish some basic ground rules before you begin a discussion. For example, agree that each of you will let the other speak without interruption. And try hard to avoid beginning any rebuttal with "but." You might also have a stipulation that each of you responds with constructive alternatives; rather than simply saying you disagree, state your reasons why and then present a viable option.

Conflict that involves abusive behavior, whether physical or emotional, extends beyond the boundaries of what is acceptable and should not be tolerated under any circumstances.

## SPOUSAL VIOLENCE

In November 1991, my partner and I were enjoying a carefree day sail in near-perfect conditions off the north coast of St. John in the U.S. Virgin Islands when we were jolted back into reality by a frantic female voice on the VHF radio. It was a woman who was clearly in distress, but it would be several long minutes before the radio operator determined what was causing her distress.

As the woman's pleas for help—a call for "Anybody, please!" —continued unabated, it became clear between her sobs and screaming that she had been physically assaulted by her partner. She said he had left the vessel in a dinghy and was driving around in circles, several hundred yards off her starboard. She could not give her vessel's position, and she was unable to recall the port they had departed from earlier that day.

The radio operator directed the woman to release the anchor in an effort to stabilize the boat's position, having confirmed earlier that the vessel was drifting and not under sail. A small child could be heard crying in the background, and the woman confirmed she had three children on board—all under five years of age. The children had not been physically harmed, but the woman had sustained a head injury and other injuries. She believed her partner would return and "kill us all." Moments later, the screaming intensified as she indicated that her partner was returning to the vessel. I turned the radio off at this point, not wanting to hear whether he killed her or not.

We learned much later that the coast guard had located the vessel and taken the injured woman and children to a safe place. Those of us listening to this drama play itself out on our radios later recalled how utterly helpless we felt, because we couldn't get a fix on her position. I still remember vividly her frantic pleas for help, and I have wondered from time to time what became of the woman and her children. I have also wondered why she would go to sea with an abusive partner.

I worked in the field of child abuse and spousal violence for more than twenty years, and I therefore understand all too well the reasons why women stay with abusive partners. Still, it is difficult to understand why any woman would place herself and her three young children in a cruising situation, as far removed from other people and helping networks as you can get.

Women who are battered on land will continue to be battered at sea; only at sea, where you are far removed from neighbors and a telephone that could save your life, the consequences could be deadly. I attempted to convey this message to Laura, age 28, when I interviewed her on her boat and she shared her concerns about going cruising.

*He doesn't mean to get angry. It's just that there are so many stressful situations [on land]. When we get away from everything and he's not so stressed, he'll be OK. I know it's hard to understand, but he was abused as a child. He's got a lot of pain inside him. I just can't abandon him. Look at the stove he installed for me; isn't it beautiful? I know he loves me, but things just get to him sometimes.*

*No, we don't have a GPS, or a sextant. We don't have an EPIRB, a VHF, or a life raft. He says we don't need those things. I'm a little afraid, but once we get away from things, we'll be fine.*

Laura is one of the few women I met during the course of my study with whom I had no further contact following our initial interview. A note I sent to her three weeks after our interview was returned and marked undeliverable. I continue to wonder what became of Laura. One thing I do believe is that she was being physically abused by her partner. But like most abused women, she believed she could change her partner if only the circumstances of their lives changed.

If you are a victim of spousal violence, don't rationalize that his abuse will cease once you are free from the stresses of land life. The sea brings a different kind of stress. When you are alone at sea, you are at his mercy—and if he's shown little on land, he will show even less at sea. Seek professional help, and until he has learned to behave in a nonabusive manner, put any thoughts about the cruising life on the back burner.

## RESPITE AND RENEWAL

Every Christmas for the past nine years, Maria and Bob—who are both in their mid-60s and have been cruising full time for ten years—check into a modest but modern resort for three days where they indulge in room service, unlimited hot showers, cable television, and 24-hour access to a telephone. It's a gift they give themselves, and one Maria describes as "the perfect present for people who have everything, like us. It's a chance to get off the boat and sample the luxuries we left behind. When we get to the point that we like them more than we do the boat, we'll look at a land base again."

Alice and Dirk, who are both in their mid-50s and have cruised full time for the past eight years, have a similar ritual, only they move from their boat in the Caribbean to a RV, or "land cruiser", in Europe each summer. They believe that variety will extend the length of time they are able to cruise without feeling deprived of other interests and activities.

Boat fatigue is much like cabin fever—that sense of claustrophobia and isolation that sets in during the depths of winter that has driven more than a few a little crazy. Whether you leave your vessel for a few days or a few months on a routine basis, time ashore can be an opportunity for respite and renewal. For some, an unhurried walk around a village and lunch on the pier is enough; for others, respite may come only from a well-deserved vacation from the boat. Some vacations can be nothing more than a day or two ashore, where you immerse yourself in the shops and cafes and the bustle of a small town or city to assuage any lingering feelings of deprivation. And letting someone else do the cooking, make the bed, and clean the bathroom can be a refreshing change.

It is often difficult for our partners and others close to us to understand why we might need respite from the boat. After all, isn't the cruising life one prolonged vacation? Yes, aspects of the cruising life can create the illusion that we are on vacation. However, the day-to-day cruising life has its own rituals—just as life on land does. Boats, like houses, require daily maintenance. Clothes require laundering, beds need to be made, heads demand cleaning. There are mouths to feed and dishes to do, and one piece of brightwork or another is always crying out for varnish. There are sails that need to be repaired, bread to bake, Christmas cards to send home, and a writing deadline to meet.

Many women take respite in annual or biannual trips home to visit grandchildren. Some routinely retreat to a land base to wait out the hurricane season, and they manage to find work or explore other interests before returning to their vessels rejuvenated and eager to venture on toward the next horizon. Some women divide their time equally between land and sea to sustain variety and prevent burnout in either lifestyle.

Taking time out from cruising for respite and renewal is a gift you can give yourself. It is a reminder that you do have choices: all you have to do is act on them.

# 7

# Leaving Life on Land: All or Nothing Is a Choice

"You can have it all. You just can't have it all at
one time."

OPRAH WINFREY

WHEN MY PARTNER AND I WENT CRUISING,
selling our home and most of our belongings was not an option I was willing to consider. Our home was little more than
bricks and mortar to my partner, but it gave me the security to
explore the cruising life at a more gradual pace. We compromised: we created an alternative to the all-or-nothing mental-
ity that seizes many who dream of going cruising. The majority
of cruising couples we have come to know also chose not to sell
out entirely.

Divesting yourselves of a land base and all but your most
precious possessions is not the only way you can realize the
cruising dream. There are many alternatives, all of which have
advantages and disadvantages. The challenge is to choose the
option that suits you best.

The majority of women I have interviewed over the years
have, with their partners, retained some type of real estate that
they managed in a variety of ways while they cruised; most were
successful with this approach, and a few were not. Some of the
women I interviewed chose not to retain a land base, which was

a choice that some of them regretted and some not. Here are some alternatives to selling out.

- Not selling out! Retaining your home and leaving it vacant (if you plan to return at regular intervals) or having family or friends house-sit.

- Renting your home, either furnished or unfurnished.

- Building a suite or apartment in your home that you can rent out to help offset costs; alternatively, you can rent out the larger portion of the house and use the suite for your own use when you are back on land.

- Downsizing and purchasing a smaller, less expensive home in a less expensive area.

- Purchasing a townhouse or condominium that requires minimal maintenance.

- Investing in a piece of property and building a garage-like structure to store your belongings.

There are many choices, but only you can decide which arrangement suits you best. In the following pages, cruising women share the pros and cons of each type of arrangement.

## RETAINING YOUR PRESENT HOUSE

If you like your present house and its location and you want to return there in your post-cruising years, then this may be a viable option for you. Having someone house-sit, or leaving the house vacant while you are away, prevents you from having to incur disconnect and reconnect costs for your telephones and utilities; your furnishings and belongings can be left as is, thus avoiding storage costs; and, your mail can be forwarded by those overseeing your property. The primary advantage to retaining a vacant house is that it is there for your personal use at any time. Also, the house is an asset that will likely appreciate, or at minimum hold its value. Some of the disadvantages of retaining your house include

- the possibility of abuse or misuse by family and friends

- your worries about wear and tear on your home and furnishings

- a vacant home is more vulnerable to break-ins and vandalism

- you remain responsible for the maintenance and financial upkeep of the property

Here are comments from women who chose to retain their homes.

*Anybody who sells out is crazy. It's your ultimate security blanket!*

*Home ownership is harder and harder to achieve these days. For most of us, our earning power decreases in our later years so we won't be able to buy another house down the road—and we most certainly won't be able to afford the cost of refurnishing it.*

*Selling the dining-room furniture for $150 makes no sense if you* *know that in five or ten years you are going to want to replace it, and then it'll cost you $1500 or more.*

*Life is full of the unexpected: you don't know when you might have to return to a home base for medical or other reasons.*

Here are comments from women who chose to sell their homes and most of their belongings.

*The only way we can afford to {buy a boat and go cruising} is to sell everything. If we don't go now, years from now I may still be sitting in this house and looking around and wondering why I'm here.*

*You've got to live for the moment. Today we're healthy and capable. In twenty years one of us could have arthritis and not be able to get in and out of the boat. We'll worry about where to live when we need to. The boat's all the real estate we want for the time being.*

*We'll rent. By the time we return to land neither of us is going to want to cut grass!*

## BEING A LONG-DISTANCE LANDLORD

Renting your house, either furnished or unfurnished, can provide enough income to offset land-based expenses, such as property taxes and, in some instances, mortgage payments. If your home is mortgage free, renting your home could generate just enough income to provide you with a nest egg when you return to land. Some couples use their rental income to subsidize their cruising lifestyle. Some retain professional property managers to oversee the house and insure the rent is collected monthly. There is a nominal fee for this service, but it eases the day-to-day responsibilities of the landlord-tenant relationship.

Here are a few of the disadvantages of renting your home.

- You are, in effect, an absentee landlord. When you get reports that the refrigerator's died or the roof is leaking, it's often difficult to determine from a distance what expenses are legitimate.

- If your tenants suddenly stop paying the rent or decide to move out, you may find yourself flying home at considerable expense to find new tenants.

- Regardless of where you are in the world, you remain connected to a major land-based investment. This distraction may prevent you from enjoying one of the primary benefits of the cruising lifestyle: the unencumbered freedom.

Here are comments from some of the women who chose to rent their houses out.

*The rent pays the mortgage and the taxes so the house supports itself.*

*We rented the entire house except for one room where we store precious things like my mother's crystal. We have a lock on the door, and our tenants respect this.*

*We arranged for a good friend to be the contact for our tenants. He's really handy and can fix things. In return, we had him down to the Caribbean for ten days on the boat with us.*

Of the women who didn't choose this option, several shared their reasoning.

*I knew I would worry about everything all the time and that would defeat the purpose {of going cruising}.*

*The last thing I wanted to do was be phoning home from all over the world to confirm the rent had been paid. And if it hadn't, then what?*

One cruising woman I interviewed chose to rent her home out, but her experience was not a positive one. She rented to a friend's son and his girlfriend. "They had two dogs, and all the furniture was covered in dog hair," she said. "The carpets had been soiled, and it took us three weeks to clean up and make repairs before we could rent again after they moved out." She would not choose this option in the future.

## BUILDING A HOME WITHIN A HOME

If your home is large enough, you may want to consider building a separate suite in it. You could have this for your use when you come back to land, or you could rent the suite out and retain the larger portion of the house for yourself.

In this arrangement, you have a space to return to if and when you need some time on land; you have a place to store your possessions; and you can generate some income from the portion of the house you rent. The disadvantages of this option are similar to those you face when you rent your entire house. And if you plan to return to land for extended periods of time, you must be psychologically prepared to share your home with strangers.

Here are comments from women who used this arrangement.

*We ended up flying home more than we had anticipated. Our son got married, I needed to have a series of medical tests, and we missed our grandchildren. It was great to have a place to stay.*

*Six months into our cruise my husband was offered a contract for six months that was just too good to turn down, so we returned to land, then we went cruising again. I'm glad we had a place all ready for us to move into—and at no cost.*

*We plan to return home regularly to take advantage of the summers and to see our grandchildren. The suite is big enough for the two of us, but too small for company—which is fine with me.*

For one woman, this arrangement was an option, but she ultimately decided against it. "It would kill me to hear strangers walking around upstairs in my house and using my things while I was tucked away in a tiny room in the basement," she said.

## DOWNSIZING

An increasing segment of the population is downsizing from large urban properties to something more modest, efficient, and affordable. Most have realized a substantial profit from selling their larger properties—in many instances, enough to buy a boat and go cruising for a few years and still maintain a smaller home base. Downsizing allows you to retain a home base on land for investment and security purposes; it provides a safety net in the event the cruising lifestyle ends sooner than you had planned; and it enables you to alternate between living on a boat and living on land. Increasing numbers of couples are choosing this option as an alternative to selling out.

The primary disadvantages of this arrangement are similar to those of retaining any land-based home. Unless you rent your property, you still have the expense of taxes, utilities, and house insurance. You will also have to pay someone to oversee your home during the periods when you're cruising.

Here is some feedback from women who chose this option.

*We were able to sell our big home in the city, pay off our boat, and buy a less expensive home two hours north of the city for less than half the selling price {of our home in the city}.*

*We still plan to spend time on land, especially during the summer months. Having a place to return to is important for us.*

*My husband wants to keep his hand in his medical practice so we want to be able to return to land for six months of the year.*

Some of the women who were not attracted to this option said

*A house is a house is a house. You still have the upkeep, the expenses, the headaches.*

*We've tucked away enough money from {selling out} to buy a house when we're ready to live on land full time again.*

## THE TOWNHOUSE/CONDOMINIUM ALTERNATIVE

Downsizing to a townhouse or condominium offers the best of all worlds for many couples. They are able to retain a mortgage-free real estate investment that makes no day-to-day maintenance demands, and the close proximity of neighbors coupled with an in-house security system alleviates most worries. The major disadvantage is that fixed expenses persist: condo fees, taxes, utilities, insurance, and so forth.

Those who downsized to a townhouse or condominium said

*This is the best of both worlds. We just lock the door and return to the boat. The neighbors know we're gone, and they keep an eye on things. They know how to reach us if there's a problem.*

*I don't worry about cutting the grass or the roof leaking. We're on the third floor. A neighbor down the hall comes in once a week to water the plants.*

*We knew where we wanted to live when we finally returned to land one day, but if we waited until then to buy real estate we probably wouldn't be able to afford it. So we invested in the townhouse to park our money somewhere. We go back at Christmas, and for a month or two in the summer; it works for us. I couldn't have sold everything.*

For some women, the disadvantages of owning a townhouse or condominium were similar to owning a free-standing house, best stated by one as "expensive and sure to make for sleepless nights."

## INVESTING IN VACANT LAND

Several couples invested in land before they went cruising and/or built garage-like storage sheds in which to house their belongings. For some, land ownership symbolized the anticipation of future dreams and a time for another major lifestyle change.

Land ownership is another way of protecting your investment income, if you believe the property will hold its value. You will still have to pay land taxes and will likely want to carry insurance on the contents of your shed. But your expenses are much less than if you chose to maintain a house.

Some of the women who bought property before they went cruising said

*We know that one day we'll want to return to land and we'll want to live on the water. So we bought a piece of land on a lake. If we wait until we return, we won't be able to afford the land because lakefront property is skyrocketing in price. We built a garage on the land and we store all of our things there. We've even installed a telephone. It's connected to an answering service from which we retrieve messages a few times a month.*

*It's comforting to know that we don't have all our eggs in one basket. The land will likely increase in value, so if we have to sell it, it's a good investment in the meantime.*

Some found the disadvantages of land ownership to be similar to those of retaining a home. "It's just something else to worry about," said one woman. "We have no idea where we will want to live one day," said another. For another woman, tying up capital in land was not an arrangement that suited her: "I don't like the idea of tying up capital in something that I can't liquidate immediately."

You can now see that selling out is not your only choice. Cruising couples find creative ways to leave their land lives—

### Our Way of Keeping a Foot in Two Worlds

I am a land person. (But I am becoming more and more a water person too!) My partner and I considered all of the options mentioned above; we considered the pros and cons of each and ultimately chose the option that was right for us at that point in our lives. We opted to downsize to a small house in the country.

Our house is nestled on a hillside with a long view of rolling hills and, beyond that, a large inland body of water. Our taxes are two-thirds of what we paid in the city, and our utilities are even less—which we owe to a passive solar heating system. The decision to downsize was motivated by our love for the cruising lifestyle and an enduring love for the land. Downsizing enabled us to immerse in both lifestyles, for varying lengths of time. Our goal is to live afloat half of the time and live on land for the other half. There will no doubt be times when the formula changes—for instance, when we decide to cruise for extended periods, something we both look forward to.

We deliberately chose a location that lends itself to seasonal use, and we are confident we can rent our home for several months of the year, should we choose to do so. The house was originally built as a ski chalet; with a rustic nature, it is designed to endure considerable wear and tear. We have earmarked one room for storing special possessions in case we rent the house, and this room will house an extra telephone line and answering service from which we'll retrieve messages when we are cruising.

Our move to the country represented a major lifestyle change of another sort and, perhaps ironically, has enhanced and revitalized our lives both on land and at sea in ways neither of us had anticipated.

and ways that suit their particular situation. By thoroughly discussing the various options and examining their advantages and disadvantages, you and your partner will make the decision that suits you best.

Each of us makes the choice that is right at a given time. Nothing is forever, which means your choices will change and evolve, just as your dreams do.

# 8

# Attention, Initiating Partners

"The problem for all of us, men and women, is
not to learn but to unlearn."

GLORIA STEINEM

WITH THE EXCEPTION OF THIS CHAPTER,
*Changing Course* has been written primarily for women who are
contemplating the cruising lifestyle. In the vast majority of instances, men are the initiators of the cruising life; therefore, this
chapter is for you—the initiating partner. By reading the up-
coming pages, you will gain greater insight about what this
lifestyle change means to your partner and how you can support her as she moves from land to water.

## REALITY CHECK

Since you initiated the idea of going cruising, you have a much
better sense than your partner does about the attractions of living on a boat. Before you read any further, take a few minutes
and make a list of the things that attract you to the cruising life.

You may be looking for freedom from the day-to-day grind:
no more commuting in traffic, no more lawns to cut, no more
workplace politics. You may be looking for an adventure and a
lifestyle that will let you explore new places and meet new people. You may simply want to be more self-sufficient.

After you compile your list, take a few more minutes to consider what your partner stands to gain from this lifestyle. Think from her perspective. You know what the cruising lifestyle holds for you, but have you taken the time to really think about what this lifestyle holds for her?

If she's resisting the lifestyle change you're proposing, it is probably because she feels her needs are being met on land and she sees no reason to alter her life. You may need to be her eyes and help her to see the attractions of a new way of living. Your partner will have other women to look to as well: throughout this book, cruising women talk about what drew them to a life on the water and what they gained from making that change.

**When you tell someone, "This will be good for you," you are essentially telling them that whatever they are presently doing is *not* good for them.**

I advise you, however, to be careful. When you tell someone, "This will be good for you," you are essentially telling them that whatever they are presently doing is *not* good for them.

## A LESS ENCUMBERED LIFESTYLE—FOR WHOM?

One of the most frequently stated attractions of the cruising life is the freedom it offers from the day-to-day encumbrances of land-based life. But freedom for you does not necessarily mean freedom for your partner.

While you may imagine that life on a boat will be a simpler existence with more freedom, your partner may be thinking that life afloat will be more complicated and constraining. And she has legitimate reasons to feel this way.

Consider for a moment who takes care of the domestic aspects of your life on land. Who does the laundry, shops for groceries, and prepares the majority of meals? Many of us enjoy the convenience of washing machines and dryers in our own homes. Unless your vessel is equipped with a washer and dryer, your partner will be hauling heavy loads to self-service laundries at every port of call. She'll ferry the laundry to shore in a dinghy, hoist it onto the pier (now a heavier load after its saltwater bath on the trip in), and transport it by taxi through a jungle of side streets to a hole-in-the-wall laundry where most of the machines are out of order and hot water has yet to make its debut. Suddenly a task that was a nonevent at home, squeezed in during television commercials, is now an all-day affair. Grocery shopping in foreign ports can be no less adventuresome.

Consider who in your family maintains contact with relatives, ensures that everyone receives birthday and Christmas gifts, and coordinates social obligations with family and friends. If your partner has looked after these "bothersome obligations" (as my partner calls them), then she may be wondering how she will coordinate these efforts from a boat, in a foreign country, and possibly on a reduced income.

Your domestic arrangements may be different. But if your partner routinely handles these tasks on land, she will have to find new ways to handle the same duties when you move on board a boat.

Apart from these household chores, she may also wonder how she'll maintain contact with aging or ill parents, provide support to adult children, maintain a presence in the lives of her grandchildren, and sustain friendships with those who have always been there for her.

## TIES THAT BIND

Does your partner enjoy close relationships with friends, family members, and colleagues? How often does she talk with her mother, her sister, her best friend? Does she delight in spending time with her grandchildren? How often does she coordinate family gatherings or arrange social time with her own friends or with couples that you both know? Are her trips to the gym as much for socializing as they are for health benefits?

Very few couples are islands unto themselves; our lives are enriched by our relationships with others. If your partner has a career outside of the home, she likely has a vast network of friends and colleagues. You may not necessarily know all the individuals who have encouraged her and applauded her successes, but they are integral to her self-esteem and the sense of worth she enjoys independent of her relationship with you.

If your partner has not worked outside of the home, her relationships with family and friends are probably even stronger since it's likely she's had more time to nurture these ties. She may be the pillar of your combined families, the one person everyone turns to when they need someone to confide in.

Women who don't work outside the home are usually more emotionally invested in their homes, their families, and their communities. What represents little more than bricks and mortar to you may very well be a peaceful sanctuary to your partner —and a place where she's invested considerable creative efforts.

For many women, the cruising life represents a loss of the vital relationships that have long enriched their lives. In my experience, most males do not experience the intensity of relationships with family and friends to the same extent as most women. One cruising woman I interviewed shared the following story about the depth of her friendships and the implications of their loss.

*For more than twenty years I have belonged to a book club that brings eighteen of us together every week. We celebrate each other's birthdays, draw names for Christmas gifts, attend the wedding showers of one or the other's children, attend baby showers for grandchildren. We are a family in many ways.*

*When [my husband] pressed me to go cruising, I knew I would miss my book club friends. But I had no idea how much until my birthday came and went and he didn't even*

**"W**hen [my husband] pressed me to go cruising, I knew I would miss my book club friends. But I had no idea how much until my birthday came and went and he didn't even acknowledge it."

*acknowledge it. Then came Christmas and he said we didn't need to exchange gifts since we had no room for anything else on the boat. He couldn't understand why I missed my friends so much and ridiculed me for sending them so many postcards.*

*We had been gone almost eight months when I decided I'd had enough of him. My friends back home seemed to appreciate me more than he did.*

If maintaining contact with family and friends is important to your partner, there are several things you can do to help her maintain those relationships from a boat.

- Install an SSB and/or ham radio and encourage your partner to learn to transmit so she feels linked to the outside world. Encouraging her to secure a ham operator's license will boost her self-confidence.

- Install one of the latest satellite telephone systems that permits long-distance communication at less than $1 a minute. This same system is e-mail ready, and the cost of sending and receiving mail is considerably less.

- Purchase a laptop computer that can be used to send and receive e-mail, both from on board and from land-based cyber cafés.

- If onboard communications systems are not affordable, encourage your partner to use telephones on shore to stay in touch with close family and friends; the costs are negligible in the long run.

- Encourage your partner to fly home once or twice a year to reestablish contact with family and friends.

- Encourage your partner to invite family members and close friends to join you in various ports along the way.

- Establish mail drops before you leave land so that correspondence from family and friends is waiting for you upon your arrival.

- Reinforce your partner's efforts to maintain a presence in the lives of grandchildren (and others) by encouraging her to send postcards and gifts for special occasions.

## DO YOU ENJOY AN EQUAL PARTNERSHIP?

Would you characterize your relationship as an equal partnership? Think about the decisions you make in your day-to-day lives. Are most major decisions made jointly? Who, for example, chose your last automobile? Who chose your most recent land-based residence—both the house as well as the town or city you reside in? Who chose your last vacation destination?

Do you and your partner combine your respective earnings and have equal access to these? Are you generally supportive of, indifferent to, or critical of your partner's spending decisions? Do you monitor how much money your partner spends on groceries, clothes, and gifts? (Are you thinking, "What's wrong with monitoring how she spends *my* money?" If you are, you need to reflect on your definition of a partnership.)

When it comes to your cruising boat, have you both played an active role in selecting the vessel? If you've already purchased your cruising vessel (or you are in the process of doing so), did your partner have an active role in the choice?

You might argue that your partner, if she's not an experienced boater, is not qualified to influence such a major decision. But this should not minimize her role in your choice of boat and how it's outfitted. The more involved she is in the selection of the vessel, the greater the likelihood is that she'll enjoy living on it.

My partner understood this. The moment I saw *Red Witch*, our motor cruiser, I knew intuitively this boat was meant for us. I didn't have a lot of knowledge about boats, but I knew—and my partner concurred with my gut reaction. He trusted my intuition and knew that if I felt this boat was right for us, I was more likely to enjoy living on a boat. I left it up to my partner to provide the logic for or against my preference; if he had indicated this particular boat was not perfect for us, for any number of sound reasons, I would have respected that. But my instinct was right, and *Red Witch* was perfect for our life afloat.

A good partnership is crucial to the cruising life; it will affect the amount of pleasure you both derive from your life on the water. Your partner will feel more a part of your life on board if she has an equal hand in creating that new existence.

In an equal partnership, it is not simply a case of listening to each other's ideas, but also being sensitive to each other's needs in this new environment, as this next section will explain.

### THE IMPORTANCE OF RESPITE ON LAND

Consider how you might respond in the following situation. You and your partner embarked upon the cruising lifestyle six months ago and have spent much of that time passagemaking in order to make a specific destination before the weather turns. While en route you experienced a few spells of nasty weather, and you are both relieved to finally reach your destination. The day you arrive in port, wet and tired after a three-day run in rain and fog, your partner discovers a nearby luxury resort and suggests splurging for a night or two on shore, to enjoy unlimited hot water and cable TV and meals cooked by someone else.

> "**When your partner does something for you that you know he would not choose to do for himself, you realize all over again how much he cares about you.**"
>
> MARY

What would your answer be to this suggestion? Would you immediately reject the idea, citing your budget is too limited for such indulgences? You may have legitimate concerns about leaving your vessel unattended so soon after arriving in a foreign port. But if you reject her idea outright without a good reason, you risk sending the message that you are more concerned about the boat's needs than you are about her needs.

Countless women have cited this very situation as an example of how they felt their partners were indifferent to and/or insensitive to their needs. Fortunately, I have also heard some women tell me how grateful they were to have partners who were concerned enough about their feelings and needs to support their suggestion for a night or two ashore—even though their partners would have preferred to stay on the boat. Mary is one such woman.

*We were exhausted after ten days at sea. The weather window we set off in had vanished a few days out. Two of the hatches leaked. The mattresses and bedding were drenched in salt water. By the time we made it to port all I wanted was twelve hours of undisturbed sleep, a warm dry bed, and anything cooked by anyone other than myself.*

*I knew Ben would be reluctant to leave the boat anchored in a strange harbor, but he said, "Count me in." I have never forgotten that. When your partner does something for you that you know he would not choose to do for himself, you realize all over again how much he cares about you.*

I'm not suggesting that your partner have her way in all your decision making or that you always put her needs before your own: that does not constitute an equal partnership. But if you have the final say in most matters and your needs are the primary impetus for most of your decisions, that does not constitute a partnership either. An equal partnership characterized by mutual respect and positive regard is a fundamental ingredient for a happy relationship and a successful cruising life. If your partner feels that you are insensitive to or indifferent to her needs, if she feels dominated by you, or if she feels that you don't respect her opinions in most matters, then she will resist going to sea with you.

### TIPS FOR BUILDING A BETTER CRUISING PARTNERSHIP

As long as the lifestyle you are proposing is perceived by your partner as *your* plan and *your* dream, her perception of herself as an equal partner in the cruising life will not materialize. And if she is not an equal partner in the plan, she is unlikely to invest emotionally in this new life. Without her emotional investment, your cruising days are numbered—if in fact you even get off the dock! There are a number of things you can do to promote her emotional investment in the cruising life. Here are some suggestions.

- Reassure your partner that she is an integral part of your cruising dream and that you will not pursue that dream

without her. Many women fear their partners will leave
them if the women don't immediately support their partners' dreams. While they may grudgingly go along with it
initially, this often leads to resentment, bitterness, and
eventually one or both of them returning to land.

- Convey to your partner that she is more important to you
  than the boat or the cruising life. And if you do not value
  her more than either, do not encourage her to leave land!

- Demonstrate an understanding of your partner's perceived
  losses. When she moves on board, it is natural for her to
  grieve the loss of family, friends, her job, and a home and
  neighborhood where she felt comfortable. Regardless of
  how insignificant you may perceive her losses to be, they are
  uppermost in her mind and heart.

- Involve her in all aspects of planning the lifestyle you are
  proposing by eliciting her opinion in all matters. If she says
  she doesn't have an opinion, don't believe her. All of us have
  opinions on everything! By encouraging her to share her
  thoughts and feelings about all aspects of the cruising life,
  you will derive a better understanding of her fears and anxieties. Consequently, you'll be better equipped to help her
  overcome those fears.

- Encourage her active involvement in all aspects of the
  decision-making process including the choice of vessel,
  the selection of equipment, the choice of a departure date,
  destinations, and so forth.

- Do not undertake vessel renovations without her involvement in the design and the choice of materials.

- Don't assume she doesn't want to be involved in any aspect of planning this lifestyle change. She may not feel confident in rendering her opinion or engaging in certain activities; your job is to encourage and support her involvement.

- Support, encourage, and reinforce all of your partner's efforts to learn—regardless of how insignificant you may perceive them to be.

- Encourage your partner to research different types of vessels and gear. When she goes to the trouble of comparing safety harnesses, for example, and then recommends a choice, heed her recommendation unless you have a compelling reason not to. If you ask her to seek out information and then make a choice independent of her efforts, and in the absence of discussion about the options, you are undermining her importance in the entire venture.

- Applaud your partner's successes and encourage the discoveries she makes about herself. She will discover talents that she never knew she had on land. Each discovery will increase her self-confidence, propel her to learn more, and reinforce her decision to embark upon the cruising life.

- Encourage her to learn how to sail your boat and help her learn how to singlehand it. There is always the remote possibility that you'll become injured during a passage and unable to help her.

- Support her need to explore ashore and/or remain in port for a longer duration. One of the primary attractions of the cruising life is the opportunity it affords to meet new people, learn about other cultures, and explore geographic and historical wonders on shore.

- Respect your partner's intuitive knowledge—especially as it relates to weather and situations when she feels unsafe.

- Take steps to ensure that your partner is not solely dependent on you financially. This may entail establishing a separate cruising kitty for her. She can use this for purchasing items that she considers important. If one of your partner's concerns about going cruising is that she won't be able to fly home if she needs to, ensure that her kitty contains the funds for a flight home.

- Reinforce your equal roles as admiral (hers) and captain (yours)—or vice versa. You cannot be both!

- Do not omit her name from your boat's business cards. If you identify yourself as captain, then identify her as the admiral. (The first mate is the four-legged mascot you may have on board.)

- Respect her degree of readiness to partake in the lifestyle change you are proposing. Since you initiated the change, you have had more time to prepare emotionally for this change.

- Applaud her efforts in the galley. Appreciate that she is adjusting to a smaller space with far fewer tools than were available in her land-based kitchen.

- Initiate dinner on shore to give her a break from the galley (without her having to suggest it first).

- Don't yell. And if you do, apologize immediately and take time later to debrief. Reassure her that it was the situation that got you upset, and not her.

- Strive to understand your partner before making yourself understood. This approach alone will go far in helping you sustain an equitable and mutually rewarding partnership.

A commitment to the concept and practice of an equal partnership is the first step toward encouraging your partner to support the lifestyle change you are proposing. In order for her to embrace the idea of life on a boat and perceive your cruising dream as one in which you will both share equally, you've got to walk your talk as well!

## SO HOW DO I *MAKE* HER GO CRUISING?

A few years ago, I participated in a seminar for would-be cruisers with approximately 40 other men and women. Most attended with their partners, but a few did not. During the question-and-answer period that followed the presentation on cruising destinations, an elderly chap stood up and said, "This is all fine and dandy but how do I make my wife get on the boat? She won't have anything to do with it!"

A number of participants offered suggestions and asked questions. As he responded to their queries, I concluded that I probably wouldn't get on a boat with this fellow either. The impatient and sarcastic overtones in his voice made me suspect he was probably difficult to live with on land. It was obvious that he was not a good listener, and he frequently raised his voice sharply when defending his efforts to, "make her go."

More revealing, however, were his references to "his boat" and the number of times he undermined the value of his wife's life on land. He stated, "We don't have anything to stay there for. The kids have their own lives and don't bother with us much. She volunteers at the library, but it's not a real job or anything. The boat's got everything we need." That statement prompted me to ask him, "Does your wife believe the boat has everything *she* needs?" He retorted, "She's never been on it in all the years I've owned it!"

Here was a man who knew he wanted to go cruising. But it never occurred to him that his partner had a land-based life from which she probably derived considerable benefit. Nor did it occur to him that she may have had legitimate reasons for not wanting to live on *his* boat. He was completely consumed with his wants and needs and could not imagine that his wife had her own wants and needs.

So how do you *make* your partner go cruising? You don't. You can't make anybody do anything they don't want to, at least not for any length of time. If you consistently try to do so, you will be perceived as bullying, dominating, and controlling.

Stop trying to make her think the cruising life is the best thing that could happen to her. Concentrate instead on understanding her needs from her perspective; then explore with her whether or not those needs could be met on a boat. You will influence your partner most by conveying a sincere interest and concern for what she wants, independent of what you want.

You can't expect her to embrace your proposal to go cruising overnight. You've had time to nurture the idea of cruising; perhaps you've dreamed about this since you were young. She may have no knowledge of what life on a boat is like.

## HOW TO ENCOURAGE YOUR PARTNER
### TOWARD THE CRUISING LIFE

Here are some tips that can help you encourage your partner to go cruising, provided you are sincere in your efforts and you genuinely care about her happiness as much as your own.

- Whether you already own a vessel or not, consider chartering a boat for a week or two (just the two of you) in an idyllic area such as the British Virgin Islands. In the BVI, the cruising conditions are safe, pristine, and what dreams are made of. This will give the two of you an opportunity to experience the romance of cruising and have time alone on a boat. If you already own a boat, use this as an opportunity to compare how the charterboat differs from your own. When you are on shore, take time to examine other vessels in the charter fleet. Most charterboat companies will allow you to board their fleet and look around inside, if the vessels are not in use. Urge your partner to identify what she likes and does not like in each vessel; ask her how she would change vital features.

- If a week or two of chartering is beyond your budget, consider attending one of the large dockside boat shows that are held regularly throughout the country.

- Listen carefully to what your partner says she needs in a vessel. Barring financial limitations, try to incorporate her needs. For example, if she needs more space and storage area than there is on that racing boat you've got your eye on, you will have to decide which is more important: living on a sleek racing boat alone or living on a slower but more spacious cruising boat with her.

- Take time to talk with your partner about her dreams. Consider how her dreams and your dreams can be integrated. One of my dreams is to bicycle through Europe. My partner suggested we do this and use our vessel as a floating hotel. He assured me that my dreams were as important to him as his own.

- Don't tell your partner what she can and cannot take aboard the boat. She is an adult and capable of discovering for herself whether or not her choices are appropriate.

- Bite your tongue every time you are tempted to say, "We can't afford it" when she wants to purchase something for herself, for someone else, or for the boat. Having an agreed-upon budget that you review together on a regular basis will prevent serious budget overrides. Nothing will extinguish her flame faster than a feeling of deprivation precipitated by your objection to nearly every purchase she tries to make.

    Likewise, don't give her *Voyaging on a Small Income* by Annie Hill for Christmas or her birthday (as my partner did). Hill's book is an excellent resource for couples wanting to cruise on a very limited income. To some, however, it portrays the cruising lifestyle as one of minimal subsistence and deprivation—and your partner's not likely to leave land for that kind of life! A better idea is to let her discover the book on her own while she's browsing in a marine bookstore.

## ARE YOU SURE YOU WANT HER TO GO CRUISING?

A few months ago I had a telephone call from a fellow who was planning to charter a bareboat in the British Virgin Islands with three other fellows. He called looking for general information, for he had heard that my partner and I knew the islands well after having sailed those waters for more than twelve years.

As the conversation progressed, he told me how he dreamed of retiring on a sailboat but that his wife loathed sailing. I was saddened by his story and asked if he had ever sailed in the BVI with his wife. "No. Several years ago I introduced her to sailing by chartering a boat on Lake Ontario for a few weeks, with the hope that she'd like it," he said. "Shame on you," I said.

"Are you sure that you really wanted her to go cruising with you one day?" He was momentarily speechless, so I explained that if my partner had introduced me to sailing on Lake Ontario, I might have had the same reaction!

**If you are sincere in wanting your partner to join you in the cruising life, then you want to do everything you can to make the lifestyle attractive.**

If you are sincere in wanting your partner to join you in the cruising life, then you want to do everything you can to make the lifestyle attractive. If she has little or no prior sailing experience, or perhaps harbors a fear of the water, introduce her to sailing in the BVI or someplace equally idyllic. You will have a better chance of encouraging her toward cruising in a warm, sunny place with crystal-clear water than in the dark, frigid, and often unpredictable waters of Lake Ontario. You want to show her the best the lifestyle has to offer— not the worst!

## IS YOUR CRUISING DREAM HER NIGHTMARE?

You may be perfectly content to eat beans out of a can on the aft deck and sleep in a lumpy old sleeping bag. Your partner may want to sit down to eat at a cloth-covered table with candles and wine in crystal goblets and sleep in sheets under a duvet. Your vision of cruising might be camping on the water; hers might be living in a floating five-star hotel. And while you might live for blue-water sailing, your partner may only see time offshore as something she has to endure in order to get to the next port.

Are your individual visions of the cruising lifestyle similar, or do you each have a very different image of what your life on the water will be like? Discuss your ideas and expectations, and decide both how you want to live and where you want to sail.

Picking your cruising destinations may sound rudimentary, but one couple I met set out with opposite goals. He was determined to explore the Arctic, and she was just as determined to head south. After a few months of cruising in a snowmobile suit and watching for icebergs 24 hours a day, she concluded that this life was not what she had envisioned and returned to land.

What if you can't find common ground? That's what Mary and Karl discovered.

Mary explained how she and her husband both had a keen interest in traveling to parts of the world that were off the beaten track. But as they began to plan a two-year sabbatical, it became apparent that their respective definitions of travel were different. Mary was making plans to go on a series of archaeological digs, which would keep her based in one port for several months. Her partner Karl desired nothing more than a few days' rest in port before heading off for the next country.

Karl is currently circumnavigating the globe on his own, taking on crew for various legs of his passage. Mary is spending her sabbatical on an archaeological dig in Europe. She and Karl plan to meet every four months to share tales of their adventures. They are both confident they will pick up where they left off after Karl completes his circumnavigation.

There are dozens of fellows living their cruising dream alone—but living alone on a boat was not the life they envisioned. Most of these men were abandoned along the way by their partner. Some were so impatient to set sail that they set off alone—having made a choice to put their needs before their partner's readiness. Most of the men who left alone now wonder why they were in such a hurry to go nowhere in particular by themselves.

You might find one of these fellows as you reach different ports along the way. He is the unshaven, somewhat emaciated-looking fellow sitting at the bar at happy hour. He might tell you that, "She simply couldn't adjust to the cruising life," but don't believe him. It was his inability to make the transition from his dream to their dream by way of an equal partnership.

If you truly want to share the cruising dream with your partner, you must be willing to make adjustments and compromises and explore alternatives. It's important that you take time to explore with your partner what her needs are and how these can be met on a boat. Her anxieties will be soothed if she believes that her happiness is as important to you as your own is.

It may take you several months or several years to create a plan for a lifestyle change that you both agree on. But you will emerge from the process with a more equitable and enriched relationship. Both of you will derive more benefit from the cruising life. And you won't find yourself holed up in a bar somewhere, drinking away your losses.

# 9

# Sixty-Four Ways to Make Cruising More Rewarding

What the cruising lifestyle brings us depends a
great deal on what we bring to the cruising
lifestyle.

WHETHER YOU'RE JUST TALKING ABOUT
going cruising, about to buy your boat, or already underway,
there are a variety of things you can do to enhance your life
afloat. Here are 64 suggestions from women who embraced the
cruising lifestyle. Some are small suggestions (did you think of
adding the deluxe travel version of Scrabble to your mandatory
gear on board?) and some are suggestions that will have a bigger impact on your cruising life, such as getting your ham radio license and learning to operate your dinghy. They are all
wise tips from women cruisers young and old that will make
your time on board happier, safer, and more rewarding.

1. Join your local sailing or yacht club. You'll expose yourself
   to people who have sailed around the world or people
   who—like your partner—dream of doing so. Being in the
   company of others who have lived on a boat, or hope to
   someday, may inspire you to ask questions. Yacht clubs and
   local cruising associations usually meet regularly, and many
   host a variety of informative presentations.

2. If you don't like camping, don't camp! Think of your boat as your home and invest in it that way—regardless of how long you plan to live aboard. Forget sleeping bags, plastic dishes, and aluminum pots! If caffè latte in the morning is your weakness, put a stovetop espresso maker and a stainless milk frother aboard. Invest in a few sets of good bed linens and a duvet and cover. Purchase cloth place mats and napkins. Invest in glass or stoneware dinnerware (Corelle, by Corning, is an all-time favorite), and take along your crystal wine glasses.

3. Hang artwork or pictures of family and friends in your saloon and/or pilothouse. Consider mounting a cork board on a blank wall where you can post lists, photographs, maps, and boat cards.

4. Enroll in a sailing course with your partner—even if he already knows how to sail. Placing both of you in the role of student tends to neutralize skill differences. Your partner's exposure to the sailing instructor's teaching style and methods of interaction will (hopefully) make him a more patient and supportive teacher with you.

5. Enroll in a sailing course *without* your partner. Regardless of how skilled and patient your partner may be, your confidence will grow tenfold by seeking instruction in the company of strangers whose skills more closely resemble your own.

6. Be sure your sailing instructor teaches you how to perform crew-overboard recovery techniques. Try them out on your own vessel.

7. Subscribe to one or two monthly sailing and/or cruising

periodicals that report on the lifestyle and technical issues of interest to cruisers.

8.  Learn how to tie a clove hitch.

9.  Join the Seven Seas Cruising Association. For a nominal fee you will receive monthly bulletins from cruisers around the world that include invaluable information about customs, marinas, preferred ports of call, areas to avoid, and other practical advice.

10. If your fear of wind, water, or waves persists, consider chartering a sailboat in the British Virgin Islands. The cruising waters here are considered the safest in the world. If this experience doesn't entice you to try the cruising life, nothing will!

11. Read *Sell Up and Sail Away* by Laurel and Bill Cooper, as well as their *Waterways of France*. The Coopers lived aboard their sailboat for a number of years before retiring to a barge, on which they continue to explore the canals of Europe.

12. Obtain your ham radio license. You will need to learn Morse code in order to transmit a brief message as part of the exam, but don't let that deter you. You'll derive a tremendous sense of achievement from passing the exam and in knowing that you are a member of the elite few who were brave enough to tackle this.

13. Start a journal. Use it to capture your thoughts, feelings, and observations about people and places you encounter along the way. You don't have to make daily entries: make notes when the urge strikes you. My journal is a hodge-podge of thoughts, feelings, and observations about every-

thing from the weather, where we spent the night, anchoring conditions, names of people and boats we've met, and so forth. I also use my journal to keep track of our expenditures and when we retrieve telephone and e-mail correspondence.

14. Compile a correspondence box to keep on board that contains extra writing journals, plenty of blank paper, envelopes, pens, a box of decorative cards (to use in a pinch for special occasions), computer paper, and spare cartridges for your printer (if you have one).

15. Make a list of provisions that you do not want to be without. Stock up accordingly before you voyage off to remote and foreign lands.

16. Keep a written inventory of provisions on board and post it in the galley. Add and subtract items as you use them and replenish your supply.

17. Learn how to tie a reef knot.

18. Learn to launch the dinghy, start the motor, and land the dinghy on shore. Learning how to operate your dinghy can be as liberating as when you first learned how to drive a car!

19. Buy your own copy of Beth Leonard's *The Voyager's Handbook*. This book is jammed full of ideas, tips, and techniques that will enhance any long-distance voyaging you may do.

20. If you don't know how to swim, take swimming lessons. At the minimum, learn how to tread water! While taking your lessons, don a pair of flippers and a snorkel and mask and ask for a few snorkeling tips.

21. Purchase a good-quality set of snorkeling gear (mask, snorkel, and fins) and reef walker shoes before you sail south. You can always wear a life vest when you snorkel.

22. Learn basic and advanced first aid and take CPR certification. You will be doing both yourself and other cruisers a favor.

23. Begin building your own cruising kitty for special indulgences. You might want to treat yourself and your partner to a lavish dinner out at an internationally renowned restaurant on your anniversary. Biras Creek Restaurant—situated on the British Virgin Island of Virgin Gorda, in North Sound—is a place whose ambiance and gourmet fare will linger long after you've sailed off. But start saving now!

24. Take a basic sewing course, if you do not already know how to sew. You may have little interest in sewing at present, but in time, you might gain a great sense of accomplishment from making items for yourself and others.

25. Invest in a sewing machine and a box of basic supplies (scissors, thread, extra needles, etc.). You'll use these to mend clothes and repair sails. You're also likely to come across beautiful fabrics—and you'll be glad you have the means to whip up a simple and elegant sarong.

26. Take a basic boating course. You will learn essential information about the different aspects of boating. An added benefit will be meeting other boaters and would-be cruisers with whom you can exchange information.

27. If you have not yet gone cruising, attend the annual Sail Expo symposium or Strictly Sail boat shows in the city nearest you. You will find seminars, workshops, and panel

discussions focusing on technical and lifestyle issues that are especially interesting for would-be cruisers. In addition to the seminars, there are hundreds of vendors selling equipment and gear, often at special boat show prices.

28. Learn to tie a bowline. If you decide to learn only one knot, make it this one: it could save your life (and maybe that of your dinghy or kayak).

29. Consider purchasing a kayak if you're planning to cruise in a warm-water area. You can head to shore on your own in this "second car," and it's easier and safer to land on a beach than a dinghy, is environmentally friendly, and an excellent way to get exercise. I use my kayak to take the dog ashore in the early hours of the morning. I can do this quietly and without disturbing those who are anchored nearby. I also use my kayak to spot my partner when he's fishing. This enables him to get dinner up and out of the water before attracting fish that are too big for the plate.

30. Learn how to use a computer, including how to send and receive e-mail. If you are not initially equipped to send and receive e-mail on board, you can always take your laptop ashore and ask to use a telephone line.

31. Buy your computer gear and learn how to operate it *before* sailing off for distant and remote destinations. Don't expect to find software and hardware support in lesser developed countries.

32. Purchase your own Leatherman, a pocket-sized multitool, and keep it on your person when you're under sail.

33. If your partner does not have his own Leatherman, add it to his Christmas list.

34. Take a photography course.

35. Buy a good camera. Before sailing off, purchase several spare batteries and a couple dozen rolls of film. You'll pay dearly for batteries and film once you leave the mainland—if in fact you can find them.

36. Have business cards for your boat printed up before you leave to share with fellow cruisers you meet along the way. We've found boat cards an excellent way for remembering the people we've met and hope to meet again.

37. Have several T-shirts for you and your partner embroidered with your vessel's name. You might want to have a couple of caps made as well. Keep extra T-shirts and hats on hand to give to guests as a souvenir of their time aboard.

38. Acquire lightweight backpacks for you and your partner that can be used for transporting groceries, hiking, and/or simply carrying what you'd normally carry in a purse. Backpacks are less cumbersome and more comfortable than a purse, and they hold far more necessities.

39. If you plan to spend a significant amount of time cruising in warmer regions (i.e., the Caribbean, South Pacific, Baja, etc.) pack at least a dozen of the lightest weight, oversized, cotton T-shirts you can find. These are as invaluable as zippered plastic bags and have multiple uses. In addition to serving as a quick cover-up when you're in port, they make great casual dresses. In a pinch, your partner can wear one if all of his have been relegated to the laundry.

40. Make a list of potential bon-voyage presents you would not mind receiving from well-wishing friends and family. Your adult children and/or closest friends may host a farewell

party for you. Whether you want them to or not, they will in all likelihood give you presents. Don't be embarrassed to make suggestions; you sold the Blue Mountain Pottery at a yard sale and surely don't want any on the boat!

41. Add the deluxe travel version of Scrabble and the current edition of the Scrabble dictionary to your bon-voyage list.

42. Add an extra-large, wooden salad bowl to your list. It does double duty for rising bread dough.

43. Make a list of all the books you've wanted to read and take the top two dozen on your list along with you. Start compiling your list now. You can never have too many books on board! You can exchange them with other cruisers or take them ashore to informal book-exchange centers. I write "Compliments of s/v *Beedahbun*" on the inside cover of every book that leaves our boat, in anticipation of running into someone who has found one of our treasures in his or her travels.

44. Purchase the best combination safety harness–life vest (self-inflating) you can find. This is one item you do not want to economize on: your life may depend on it.

45. Learn how to read charts and plot a course.

46. Learn how to operate the GPS and familiarize yourself with its crew-overboard function.

47. If you are concerned about how you will fill your time once you begin cruising, consider signing up for a self-study or correspondence course that you can complete at your leisure. The list of academic and general interest courses that can be done at a distance is endless. One woman I in-

terviewed took a series of courses to upgrade her knowledge in a work field she hoped to enter at a future date.
Another took along a three-part wine appreciation course
that she completed over a two-year period (it came in handy
when she toured the vineyards of South America with her
partner!).

48. Learn a second language (Spanish and French are cruisers'
languages of choice).

49. Take time to reflect on what you hope to gain from the
cruising life. Note and date your reflections in your journal. These could be specific goals, such as becoming a more
confident sailor, passing the ham radio exam, or learning
to identify the major constellations. They could also be very
broad efforts, such as learning to relax more or exploring
your spiritual side.

50. Take along your pet, or pick up a stray along the way. My
choice is a dog, but many cruisers have a cat on board. Some
even have birds. Pets, like children, keep us connected to
other similarly inclined people. In the case of dogs, they
keep us connected to the land. Yes, there are some countries
that do not allow pets on shore without obtaining a permit
beforehand, and some countries demand a period of quaran-
tine. The French, Dutch, and U.S. islands welcome pets as
long as vaccinations are up to date. And contrary to what
many people believe, the British Virgin Islands allow dogs
(and cats) to enter, as long as a permit is obtained in advance. Be sure to find out which countries are dog- and cat-
friendly and which are not before you sail off.

51. Don't compromise on your dinghy. This is your car. You
want it to be easy to start, easy to pull onto a beach, and fast

enough to cut through waves and get you to the distant nooks and crannies you will want to explore. Hard-bottom dinghies are preferred by most cruisers because they cut through the waves rather than pound on them. However, hard bottoms are very heavy, and you need two people to pull one high up on to the beach. You also can't deflate a hard bottom and stow it below deck, as you can a soft bottom.

52. Don't compromise on the dinghy motor. We've seen more hard-bottom dinghies being propelled by a 6-horsepower engine or less—and almost everyone regrets the investment. An 8-horsepower engine is good; depending on the size and make of the dinghy, a 9- to 15-horsepower motor is better.

53. Purchase a book on how to identify constellations. This will make your nighttime watches more interesting. When you are at anchor on a starry night, you can challenge your partner to see who can identify the most constellations.

54. Purchase glass baking dishes instead of aluminum. They're easier to clean and don't rust.

55. Add a nonstick frying pan to your tool kit. Add a wok, too. They'll reduce galley duty substantially.

56. Choose dark, lightweight linens (towels, sheets, etc.) for their ability to attract heat and their ability to dry quicker when you hang them on your boat or take them to a commercial laundry. It's almost impossible to rid thick velour beach towels of sand and salt water.

57. Add a pressure cooker to your repertoire of utensils. I resisted this tool for years, due to a fear of blowing a hole in

the roof. My fears were unfounded, however: today's models come equipped with foolproof safety features.

58. To reduce the chances of bringing bugs aboard, wash all fresh produce you bring on board immediately in a solution of liquid bleach and water. You need only add a teaspoon of bleach to a half liter or so of fresh water. Immerse the item quickly and dry it off with a clean cloth. This form of bug control, albeit a little time-consuming, is a virtual insurance policy for keeping your boat roach free.

59. Continue your roach prevention program by keeping cardboard off your vessel. Roaches like to lay eggs under the flaps (where they feed off the glue). When it's easier to haul supplies in cardboard boxes, leave them in your dinghy or on the pier. Some cruisers remove labels from cans and mark their contents with a permanent marker to avoid bringing roaches aboard (again because of the glue under the labels).

60. Even if you don't have roaches on board, place a few roach traps in inconspicuous spots throughout the cabin as a preventive measure. And always set out roach and ant traps when you lay the boat up on land.

61. To ease congestion in the galley when you have guests aboard, keep a cooler on deck stocked with cold drinks. This will keep many hands from opening the icebox every fifteen minutes and allowing precious cold air to escape. Assign ice duty to one of the mates and make it their responsibility to purchase ice along the way. They will feel better for having made a contribution—and running out of ice is no longer your worry!

62. When guests ask, "What can we bring?" tell them to bring along a beach towel. They will assume greater responsibility

for ensuring *their* towels make it back to the boat after a frolic on the beach, and they'll make sure their towels are hung on the rails to dry and they go home with them— rather than to the self-service laundry with you.

63. Post a laminated notice in the head advising users what can and cannot go into your marine toilet. Don't assume everyone knows what not to throw into the toilet. You might also want to add operating instructions. Not all heads operate in an identical fashion.

64. Consider developing a "Welcome to Our Vessel" handbook or pamphlet that introduces overnight guests to your vessel and to systems your guests will use most (fresh water, head, dinghy, etc.). This is an excellent way to ease their anxieties, as well as your own.

# 10

# Because You Asked...

> "We cannot escape fear. We can only transform it
> into a companion that accompanies us on all our
> exciting adventures. Take a risk a day—one
> small or bold stroke that will make you feel
> great once you have done it."
>
> SUSAN JEFFERS

WHEN MY PARTNER AND I BEGAN PLANNING
our lifestyle change, I was brimming with questions about
cruising and living aboard. I wanted practical information
about everything—from how to live in a small space to whether
or not we should tow the dinghy for overnight voyages. Some
information was easy to come by. I had read much about the
types of provisions cruisers commonly run short of first and
those that were hardest to come by outside of North America.
What I really wanted, however, was firsthand advice from cruising couples—and from women in particular.

When I began my study on the cruising lifestyle, I had a perfect opportunity to continue asking questions, to pass along
the timely tips enthusiastically shared by others, and to compare experiences. Being able to respond with confidence to some
of the questions from women who were contemplating the
cruising lifestyle represented a pivotal turning point for me: I
was now able to give back at least a little of what I had learned
from others and from my own cruising experiences.

What follows is a selection of the questions and answers that

I am most frequently asked, along with several questions that I—and other cruising women—sought answers to in our earliest stages of contemplating the cruising life.

These responses are not absolute. They only represent what I —and other cruising women—have discovered in our adventures afloat. If you have a question that does not appear here and you feel it's a topic that should be included in a future edition of this book, please write to me in care of the publisher. I will also do my best to respond to your questions personally, should you desire this.

## COMPATIBILITY

*My husband and I are opposites in many respects. Since the last of our four children left home a year or so ago our differences have become more pronounced. We don't seem to like the same things—books, music, movies. Even our friends are different. His idea of a good time is beer and pizza with a gang of people; I like a quiet evening out with another couple at a good restaurant. Recently my husband said he thinks we should rent or sell the house and go cruising for a year or two now that the kids have gone. I've just returned to the workforce after being a stay-at-home mom for twenty years and I like my work as an administrative assistant in a busy, bustling real-estate office. We have a 36-foot boat that we used to sail with the kids on weekends, but I can't imagine living on it full time! I don't think my husband and I have enough in common to go cruising. What should I do?*

It is quite common for a couple to drift apart during the child-rearing years and, in the process, develop different interests. This is especially the case when one partner has stayed home to care for children. Since you no longer have children at home, you have filled your time by returning to the workforce and are no doubt enjoying both the independence your work gives you as well as the challenge and stimulation it offers. Your husband, on the other hand, is ready for a lifestyle change—after being the primary provider for a number of years.

The fact that you don't like the same things does not mean that you don't have any common interests. Perhaps you have both been so busy that you haven't had time to rediscover the things you once enjoyed together and the things you once admired in each other. Think back to what attracted you to your mate in the first place. What sorts of things did you do together and when was the last time you did them without your children?

You do not say that you dislike sailing; rather, you aren't sure you could live aboard your particular boat. Try to identify what it is about your current vessel that you don't like; then consider how your boat might be transformed to a liveaboard vessel you'd feel comfortable on. If you come up empty, talk with your partner about trading your current vessel for one that has more appeal for you.

Your return to the workforce has special significance to you and is clearly a source of considerable fulfillment at this time. Have you explained to your husband how important your job is to you? Don't assume that he knows. He may not appreciate the significance your work has for you—especially since it's something you have only recently undertaken. Preparing a boat for cruising takes time, and many couples opt to live aboard their vessels for a period of time to adjust to life aboard and to continue earning money until they sail off. You and your partner need to develop a time line that takes into account your need to continue working (at least for the time being) and his need to work toward making a change. Taking an unpaid leave of absence from your job is another option to consider.

The cruising life has the potential to help you and your partner rediscover yourselves as individuals and as a couple—assuming you want to remain a couple. If you are uncertain about whether you want to continue a relationship with your husband, don't go cruising with him under any circumstances. If, however, you are still attracted to him and you want to invest time and effort in rejuvenating your relationship, the cruising lifestyle may provide an opportunity to do this, and more.

# DIET

*I've talked with a few women who said they grew tired of canned and processed foods while cruising. How difficult is it to find fresh produce and groceries?*

If you add provisioning and galley management to your list of skills to master, you will not have to subsist on canned and processed foods or worry about feeling deprived of fresh, nutritious fare. The key to a varied and nutritious diet is well-planned provisioning, both before you set out and at major ports along the way. Take advantage of opportunities to stock up on galley essentials and long-lasting fresh goods at the larger, less expensive markets (these can generally be found within walking distance in larger ports). You can also buy fruits and vegetables from street vendors in most small towns and villages.

Talk with other cruisers to learn which fresh foods have the longest shelf life and ask for tips on how to store those items. You'll quickly discover there is no one method for storing fresh eggs or root vegetables. For example, I swear by the cotton net hammocks that hang above the dining table in my saloon and hold lemons, limes, potatoes, onions, garlic, bananas, etc. In addition to their accessibility, the nets prevent produce from being bruised. They also allow for continuous aeration, which prevents mold and mildew from forming.

Depending on where you cruise, you will have no difficulty finding fresh produce and other food staples—but not necessarily the ones you crave most. For example, bananas, mangoes, and limes were the only fruit available at one island I recently visited; but they were fresh, inexpensive, and available in abundance. I was not able to buy fresh milk there, but I was able to purchase a case of UHT (ultra heat treated) milk; it was expensive but no less nutritious. Powdered milk is also readily available.

Don't assume that the smaller markets in small villages will be more costly than supermarket chains. We paid substantially less for capers, stewed tomatoes, and fresh milk on the island of Culebra than we did in the urban centers of Puerto Rico. We also found inexpensive frozen, boneless, skinless chicken breasts in a little store that was a 10-minute walk from a more expensive deli-style store in Sopers Hole on Tortola. Seek and you shall find!

# EXERCISE

*I'm active on land and maintain a daily exercise routine to keep fit. Will the cruising lifestyle compromise my fitness level?*

This is one aspect of the cruising life that concerned me most, since I too am committed to a daily physical fitness routine on land. With ingenuity and self-discipline, the cruising life has the potential to enhance your current level of fitness.

Our cruising routine includes having access to land each day to walk a few miles or do a serious hike. We rarely miss an opportunity to walk the length of every beach we discover—nor do we forgo walking for taxis (much to the dismay of my partner in some instances). We snorkel and swim daily, when conditions permit it, and on days that I swim, I have designed a water routine that substitutes for my workout with arm and leg weights. When you're passagemaking, weight training will keep your muscles toned until you're able to make landfall and don your hiking boots again.

Our purchase of a two-person kayak, which can be just as easily maneuvered by one person, has been especially beneficial for maintaining fitness. Kayaking tones and strengthens the upper body and lends balance to my daily walking routine. Modifying your dinghy so you can row it comfortably is another option.

## HEELING

*I'm terrified when the boat heels over. Will I ever get over this?*

Conquering my fear of heeling has been one of my biggest challenges. If it's any consolation, most people are not comfortable heeling beyond 25 degrees—not even the captain! Heeling places our bodies in an unnatural position and, in doing so, upsets our equilibrium.

Most of us are uncomfortable with heeling because we fear the boat will flip over and/or sink in the process. My partner thought he could soothe my fears by familiarizing me with the laws of physics that explain how much a vessel has to heel before it will turn over. The actual degree of heel varies from boat to boat, however, the vast majority of boats will not turn upside down (or turn turtle) until they exceed 145 degrees of heel. For the longest time, this knowledge did little more than cause me to fixate on the inclinometer (heeling meter)! I eventually learned to trust our boat.

Contrary to what many people think, most boats are most efficient at 15 to 25 degrees of heel. If the sails are properly set, this is the angle when most boats sail their fastest. When I see boats heeled over, I assume this is done to give the crew an adrenaline rush and certainly not because the vessel is going faster than it would at less heel.

To reduce your boat's angle of heel, you have to reduce sail. When you are uncomfortable, a caring and supportive partner will reduce sail without hesitating. A good rule of thumb is to put a reef in the mainsail before you set sail; it's harder to do this while you are underway in the windier conditions that warrant a reef in your sails.

With experience, you will develop your own comfort zone. My preference is 15 degrees of heel. I am comfortable at 20 degrees, but I need time to settle down when we heel 25 degrees or more. Until you find your comfort zone, keep in mind that the percentage of time you will spend heeling is minimal in the grand scheme of things.

## INSURANCE

*We plan to cruise for two to three years and do not plan to insure our boat because the annual rates will consume too large a portion of our cruising kitty. Some of our friends think we are crazy to proceed without insurance. Do most cruisers carry insurance? Are we foolish to proceed without it?*

There are solid arguments both for and against buying insurance. The first question you need to ask yourself is whether you can afford not to have insurance. Can you afford to absorb any losses, including losing your vessel outright? If everything you own is contained in your boat and the boat is your only home, you may want to consider what the ramifications would be if your home and all its contents were demolished. It happens.

Many cruisers whose uninsured vessels were completely demolished in hurricanes Hugo, Marilyn, or Georges had no alternative but to return to land and paying jobs.

We have met many couples who self-insure, which means they are prepared (at least psychologically) to absorb the cost of any harm their vessel may sustain. Many self-insured couples argue they are more attentive to factors that might harm their vessels than cruisers who carry insurance. For example, self-insured cruisers are more likely to anchor far from the crowds to avoid incurring damage.

These cruisers might also steer clear of the hurricane zones at certain times of year. We recently met a couple with a Swan 44 who decided to self-insure; they calculated that over a 10-year period, the cost of insurance would equal the purchase price of their boat. If they lost their vessel, they had the financial means to replace her immediately.

We've also met couples who insure for part of the year, when their risk of sustaining damage in a hurricane is greater.

My partner and I are firmly on the side of purchasing insurance. If we lost our vessel, we could not afford to replace her. If she were to sustain serious damage while "sitting on the hard" during a hurricane (if she was dismasted or holed by another vessel that fell on her), we could have her repaired for minimal out-of-pocket expense.

There is also the matter of your psychological comfort level. We sleep much better at night—whether we are on our boat or off it—knowing that the vessel is insured.

The issue of personal liability is another consideration. For example, if you happen to slip your anchor and do serious damage to another person's vessel who is also not insured, that owner will demand reimbursement for damages. In good faith, you must pay up. If a friend were seriously injured aboard your vessel, they might sue you. If you're not insured, you could find yourself spending a lot of time in court and spending a lot of money on litigation. Boat insurance includes coverage for these types of liabilities.

The percentage of full-time cruisers who do not have insurance is estimated to be anywhere from 40 to 75 percent. In my opinion, this is a frightening number of people who have chosen to risk losing a lifestyle they have worked hard to achieve.

Shop around. There is good coverage to be had for relatively little expense. Failing this, consider working a little longer to save the necessary funds or interrupt your cruise along the way to earn your annual insurance premiums.

# PETS

*I can't bear the thought of parting with my dog. He's been part of my life for ten years. What are the pros and cons of having pets aboard?*

There is a definite increase in the number of four-legged first mates in recent years—and their two-legged masters would not be without them. Cats are more common than dogs, primarily because they don't need to go ashore. Some cruisers have one of each and a bird to boot!

My partner and I wouldn't cruise without our nine-year-old springer spaniel, Sydney. Our only regret is that she is not eligible for frequent-flier miles! We make a point of anchoring every night so Sydney goes ashore three times a day (ideally, in the morning, midday, and in the evening). She also joins us on most hikes.

Many cruisers limit their offshore passages to 24 hours or less, so they can accommodate their dogs who will generously "hold it" until they reach shore. Cruisers who spend considerable amounts of time voyaging offshore train their dogs to do their business in a designated area or on a piece of indoor-outdoor carpeting, which they drag behind the boat for cleansing while under way.

Many cruisers without pets on board insist they left land to avoid that kind of responsibility. When they see us taking our dog ashore, they remark, "That's why I don't have a dog. They're too much work!" It's all a matter of perspective. I don't consider taking my dog ashore to be work. On the contrary, I enjoy walking, and our dog gives me a sense of security—regardless of how friendly she may seem.

When it comes to security, many cruisers say they sleep better at night knowing their dog will bark if someone tries to board their vessel. In many islands, onboard dogs are considered to be a deterrent to vandals. We have made many new friends as a result of the attention our dog draws when she howls from the bowsprit, although fewer friendly faces appear when she howls before the sun breaks the horizon.

The primary disadvantage of having a pet on board is that they are not allowed to disembark in some territories, which can restrict your cruising destinations. For example, dogs are not allowed on British territory (with the exception of the British Virgin Islands) unless they are quarantined for a very long period of time. Dogs are welcome in French, Dutch, and U.S. territories as long as you verify your pet has been vaccinated. Be sure to clarify where your pet is welcome before you set out.

Keep in mind that not all cultures are enamored of cats and dogs. With the exception of the French, most cultures won't let you bring your dog into a restaurant, supermarket, or Laundromat. Pets are best left on board for these kinds of excursions. We also encountered taxi drivers who refused to allow our dog in their vehicles—until I agreed to pay a fare equivalent to that of a third person.

The companionship of pets can be hard to live without. We recently met a couple who took pity on a female stray who had hung around their boat in Salinas, Puerto Rico, for six weeks— grateful for the scraps they threw her way. When they were ready to weigh anchor, they decided Jackie was coming along. They delayed their departure to have her inspected by a veterinarian. Jackie had heartworm, which required treatment and necessitated more time in Salinas. This turned out to be a great excuse to rent a car and tour another part of the island. She took a few weeks to find her sea legs, but Jackie has turned into an indispensable companion.

*What about the availability and/or cost of pet food?*

Pet food is available at any supermarket and at most smaller stores. We don't have to worry about the availability of dog food: we feed our dog people-food (due to allergies), and I make her biscuits. This also ensures her food is fresh, and we avoid having weevils on board and the other pests that gravitate toward dry pet food.

## READINESS

*My partner is impatient to go cruising. I'm just not ready. How do we resolve this impasse?*

In your own mind, sort out exactly what you mean by "not ready" and try to identify what needs to happen before you do feel ready to leave (assuming you anticipate being ready at a future date).

Simply saying, "I'm not ready" won't help you get ready— and it won't help your partner understand your needs. Are you in the midst of something that you need to complete, such as a university degree? Are you in the middle of a particularly challenging and stimulating project that you want to finish? Are you concerned about parents who are elderly and in poor health? Perhaps your last child left home recently, and you are experiencing a period of emotional transition you need to resolve before embarking on yet another change. Articulating your needs and developing a strategy for becoming ready to depart is almost certain to garner the support of your partner.

If you don't have a concrete reason preventing you from making a major lifestyle change, explore the possible psychological factors. You may not be ready to give up the security you derive from certain aspects of your land-based life—such as your home, career, access to family and friends, and involvement in community affairs. You may also fear certain aspects of the cruising life, such as living in a smaller space. Try reframing what you fear losing and think instead of what you stand to gain.

When you go cruising, you won't lose family and friends: you'll simply learn to communicate with them in a different way. You can also invite them to join you for a week or two in a part of the world they would not otherwise have a chance to visit. In sharing your cruising lifestyle with them, you enrich their lives as well as your own.

You might try living on your vessel for a period of time. That way, you can stay involved with land-based activities while you make the transition to life on a boat.

There are many people who will never be ready for anything. They require a little prodding or an occasional nudge to move them along. If you are this type of person, you might consider taking a risk and letting nature take its course. In other words, try it; there's a good chance you'll like it!

# SEASICKNESS

*I'm prone to severe seasickness. Any suggestions?*

In most instances, seasickness can be prevented or controlled with prescription and over-the-counter medications, in addition to a variety of natural remedies and good pretrip planning. Talk with your doctor and your pharmacist. Talk with other cruisers about natural remedies such as gingerroot (to suck on), gingersnaps (for snacking), and ginger tablets (available in health food stores). The trick is to take preventive action *before* you feel the first twinge of illness.

There are also certain strategies you can employ to reduce the severity of your discomfort. You can prepare meals before you get under way to minimize the amount of time you spend below deck. Some individuals avoid going below deck to do anything other than use the head. Others have their partner change the boat's angle of heel or ask them to heave-to so they can prepare meals and get other below-deck activities done.

In rare cases, seasickness can be so unmanageable that you might have to skip all but the shortest passages. Some women do not accompany their partners on passages that exceed a few days; they fly while their partner sails with a crew.

If you cruise with a supportive partner, exercise good planning, and curtail the duration of your passages; there is no reason why seasickness has to prevent you from enjoying the cruising life.

# SELLING OUT

*My partner is adamant about selling everything before we go cruising. He refuses to be an absentee landlord and says it makes no sense to*

*pay storage fees that will eventually cost more than our things are worth.*
*What do other women do when faced with this dilemma?*

In chapter 7, I presented a variety of alternatives to selling out. If
your partner doesn't want to be an absentee landlord, what is preventing *you* from taking on that responsibility? If you can afford to
retain your land-based home while you cruise, then there is no reason for him to object—as long as you hold up your end of the
bargain. If you agree to take on the responsibilities associated with
maintaining your land base and your partner remains adamant
about selling out, consider whether this is the type of person you
want to risk selling out for. His inflexibility and insensitivity to
your needs and capabilities will not make for happy cruising.

## WAVES

*The thought of confronting 30-foot waves scares me to death. How likely*
*is this to happen?*

If you plan your offshore voyaging carefully, which means waiting
for an appropriate weather window and voyaging during the seasons when weather is known to be fairly benign, the chances of
confronting gigantic waves are rare. Even in these circumstances,
however, there are no guarantees that you will not have a period
of rough weather—including large, 12- to 15-foot waves or swells.

When we think of waves, many of us tend to imagine a 30-
foot vertical wall towering over us. In reality, there is usually a
considerable distance between the waves. They seem more like
swells, and you can comfortably glide over them. It is only in
shallow waters when you are close to land (or bordering shallow fishing banks), or when strong winds oppose strong cur-
rents that the distance between waves is much shorter and the
height of the waves appears more menacing.

# WEATHER

*One of my fears is that we will get caught in bad weather. How likely is this to happen?*

It depends. The cruisers who are most likely to encounter bad weather are the ones who adhere to rigid time schedules that dictate which days they have to be in port—either to retrieve or drop off guests, or because they are trying to see the world in fifteen days, so to speak. With good planning and the freedom to remain in port until a good weather window opens, you may be subjected to nothing more than a light gale from time to time.

Many cruisers avoid cruising in certain regions of the world at specific times of the year when hurricanes or cyclones are most active. Research the weather patterns in the regions in which you anticipate cruising well in advance. You may find that you'll have to adjust your cruising schedule so you don't reach a desired region at the height of the stormiest season.

If you choose to cruise when the risk of encountering severe weather is greatest, stay close to a sheltered port, monitor weather stations twice daily, preselect your "hurricane hole" (the place you'll take your vessel in the event severe weather is imminent), and be sure your boat is equipped with sufficient ground tackle (extra anchors and lines).

Jimmy Cornell, author of the invaluable *World Cruising Routes*, writes this about weather:

> As a result of profound changes that have occurred in the ecological balance of the world environment, there have been several freak weather conditions that have occurred in recent years. Their most worrying aspect is that they are rarely

predicted, occur in the wrong season and often in places where they have not been known before. Violent storms have been recorded recently at times and in places where they have not occurred before. Similarly, the violence of some tropical storms exceeds almost anything that has been experienced before. The depletion of the ozone layer and the gradual warming of oceans will undoubtedly affect weather throughout the world and will increase the risk of tropical storms. The unimaginable force of mega-hurricanes Hugo and Andrew should be a warning of worse things to come. All we can do is heed those warnings, make sure that the seaworthiness of our vessels is never in doubt and, whenever possible, limit our cruising to the safe seasons.

Cornell's book has guided more people who cruise safely around the world than any other. I highly recommend it.

Bruce Van Sant, author of another worthwhile book, *The Gentleman's Guide to Passages South*, advocates unequivocally for the importance of waiting for weather. "Depart only when favorable conditions prevail and shall be sustained for a day longer than you need to make a safe harbor," he says. Van Sant's book has guided many cruisers south from Florida to Venezuela and back. Don't leave land without either of these books.

## WEIGHT GAIN–WEIGHT LOSS

*I've been told that the cruising lifestyle causes most men to lose weight and most women to gain weight. Is this true, and if so, why?*

This is true for many, but certainly not for all cruisers. Living on a boat involves a lot of manual labor and physical movement that stresses different muscle groups. The lifting, reaching, bending, stretching, pulling, pushing, and so forth tends to be done more by males than females. On land, the opposite is true. Females tend to do more of the domestic labor that requires similar exertion: lifting, stretching, reaching, scrubbing, mowing, polishing, sweeping, vacuuming, walking up and down stairs dozens of times every day, and so forth. Females perform similar activities on a boat, but there is a lot less area to cover and they therefore exert less energy in completing this work.

One activity that women tend to do more of on the boat is cook and bake. While this is an enjoyable pastime, it can also be fattening. Freshly baked bread is the worst culprit—so be forewarned! A second activity that plays havoc with women's weight is an increase in alcohol consumption. No, the cruising lifestyle doesn't drive women to drink but the socializing does. A glass or two of wine a day is unlikely to harm you; but when this is preceded by a beer or two during the heat of the day and a couple of alcohol-laden sundowners accompanied by snack foods, the pounds pile on in a very short time. Males metabolize alcohol faster than females do and similar indulgences are not as outwardly apparent. My partner loses weight when we live on our boat; I tend to hold my own or lose a pound or two. I attribute his weight loss to the fact that the cruising lifestyle demands more activity from him than our lifestyle ashore does.

The amount of food we consume on board also varies considerably from our land-based consumption. Our appetites are lessened when cruising in warm climates, and we tend to eat far more fish and rice—which are lower in calories, easier to digest, and always available.

Bear in mind that most men naturally carry more weight and

muscle than most women do, and their bodies therefore burn more calories from their exertions. The key to maintaining your weight or slimming down after you move aboard is to maintain a daily exercise routine, which should include a strength-training regime on alternate days. Choose between a couple of sundowners or glasses of wine (if this is your usual habit)—but don't indulge in both; keep snacking to a minimum; and take advantage of the ocean's bounty as often as you can.

# YELLING

*My partner's yelling intimidates and demeans me. Almost every woman I talk with says her partner yells. What gives?*

Nobody likes to be yelled at. It implies that we have in some way screwed up or, worse, that we are incompetent. Yelling as a means of telling someone what to do in a potentially danger-ous situation is one thing; yelling that is degrading and laden with criticism and disgust is nothing short of abusive. The fact that most yellers are males suggests that power and control are at the root of their yelling. More than anything, however, yelling is a means of expressing emotions that many people have not yet learned to express in more constructive and less abusive ways. When someone yells, they may be saying, "I'm stressed, I'm afraid too," or, "I don't know what to do next." Unfortu-nately, the message the yeller intends to convey is rarely the message that is received.

Tell your partner how his yelling affects you. Don't assume he knows how his behavior makes you feel. Be sure to choose an appropriate time to confront him with his behavior. Telling him, "It hurts my feelings when you talk to me this way" when he's yelling at you to take action to avoid a collision in a busy harbor is *not* the right moment. Wait until both of you are not distracted, then calmly tell him how his behavior makes you feel. Be sure to add that you don't like feeling this way all day, every day. Try to negotiate an alternative way of communicating. For example, the next time he yells in a tone of voice that humiliates or degrades you, explain how you will raise your hand and turn away until he stops. Or prepare him to hear you say, "You're yelling." This will be his cue to stop and try again.

One woman I interviewed took the drastic step of getting off the boat at their next port of call and refusing to return until her partner agreed to change his behavior. When he refused to acknowledge there was a problem, she flew home and visited her grandchildren to let him know that she was serious. Two weeks later he flew to her and promised to try very hard to stop yelling. She agreed to go back to the boat with the understanding she would leave again—perhaps permanently—if his behavior continued. He didn't change overnight. But he did reduce the number of times he yelled, and he apologized when he lost control. She felt he was making a sincere effort to change, and they continued cruising for three more years.

Many men yell when they are stressed, afraid, concerned, frustrated, or simply at a loss about what to do next in a given circumstance. Try to remember that yelling is his way of expressing emotions that he has not yet learned to express in any other way. This does not justify his behavior, but it may prevent you from taking his yelling personally.

# Nothing Is Forever

"You don't get to choose how you're going to die.
Or when. You can only decide how you're going
to live. Now."

JOAN BAEZ

WHEN MY PARTNER PROPOSED THAT WE GO
cruising, I felt as if we were going to sea and never looking
back: I interpreted my partner's desire to shift our lives to the
water as something that would last forever.

That sense of finality compounded my fears, for it seemed to
negate everything I had come to know on land. But once I discovered that the cruising lifestyle did not diminish my enjoyment of activities ashore, I began to find greater joy in living
on a boat. And I learned that these two lives—one on land and
one on the water—could in fact complement each other. If I had
known that from the outset, I might have embraced the cruising life sooner.

Some cruisers go to sea for a set duration of time; they may
plan a one-year sabbatical, or sail for as long as their pocketbook
will allow. Some set out for an indeterminate period of time,
and they plan to keep cruising as long as they are still enjoying
the lifestyle. Regardless of their intentions when they set out,
one thing is certain: cruising will not be forever. If you are de-
bating the pros and cons of making a change to the water, or if

you're already sailing and plagued by a sense of ambivalence about your choice, take comfort in knowing that land will one day beckon as strongly as the lure of the sea does now—despite what your partner might say.

Just as the sea appeals to our partners as respite from the frantic rat race, land will eventually call with enticements of another kind. Just as we are lured to faraway lands in exotic places, home will draw us back someday, for cruisers remain psychologically connected to their own backyards and to family and friends. The reality is that most cruisers find it virtually impossible to sever their land ties completely.

All cruisers mix their life on the water and their life on land in individual ways. Some actively combine a land-based and water-based existence, and they split their time between both places. For some, land is the place they return to after a long journey at sea.

There are cruisers I call liveaboard amphibians—they have a hybrid existence. They spend extended periods of time living on their boats in one port or another, and they spend extended periods exploring on land. You might find them in Baja or Samoa, in Elba, Georgetown, Luperon, and beyond. They might be drawn to land to tour ruins from ancient civilizations, participate in language immersion programs, scale mountains, visit art galleries, participate in archaeological digs, or simply comb miles and miles of silky beach. Land is where they want to be: the sea is merely the means for bringing them there.

Some couples find a way to extend their cruising lifestyle onto land, and they trade their water cruisers for RVs, or "land cruisers", as cruisers call them. You might find them "anchored" in parks throughout the nation in their land cruisers, gathered around an open fire toasting marshmallows the way they once gathered for a clambake on the beach.

Some cruisers keep a land base and return to it for part of each year. Full-time cruising friends of ours keep a chalet in the Colorado mountains. They return there in the winter for skiing and in the summer for hiking, and they refer to these land-based sojourns as vacations. They cannot imagine one lifestyle without the other.

And for some, cruising helps them to make the passage to a new kind of life on land. Armed with a renewed respect for the land and determined to practice the lessons they learned from the sea, many cruisers reestablish a land-based lifestyle with no less passion than the fervor that fueled their move to a cruising life. This is what close friends of ours, Wanda and Bert, did.

Wanda and Bert were both in their 70s when they decided to retire from their cruising life, and they looked forward to reestablishing their lives back on land with no less fervor than when they embraced the cruising lifestyle. They had lived aboard their Whitby 42 for sixteen glorious years; they were full-time cruisers for eight years, then half-time cruisers for eight years. Their decision to return full time to a land-based lifestyle was precipitated by the arrival of grandchildren, as well as a desire to pursue hobbies and interests in a more structured environment. Wanda had taken up painting when she was cruising, and she wanted the opportunity to attend art classes on a regular basis. Bert had enjoyed tennis prior to cruising, and he looked forward to joining a club.

They purchased a condo in a little village near the ocean in a southern state. They have a silver land cruiser in their parking lot, which is their home away from home for several months of the year. Wanda attributes much of the joy they are experiencing on land to the lessons she and Bert learned at sea: "respect, reuse, recycle, relax, and rejoice," as she says. Four years after returning to land, Wanda reflected on her journey from land to sea and back to land again:

*When we set out on [our boat] we were eager to leave behind the frenzy, the stress, and the mess of stuff we had accumulated over the years. We were also dispirited. We seemed to be caught in a cycle of work, spend, and splurge. More somehow seemed better. As I think about it now, I feel as if I'm talking about anyone's life but our own. We have changed so much.*

*Bert saw the cruising life as one that would rehumanize us. I wasn't at all sure what he was talking about. But I thought, "If this is what it'll take to get him to slow down, then I'm game." In truth I was scared to death.*

*Well, all I can tell you is that neither one of us is the same person we used to be. It's as if our minds underwent a major readjustment. We were reborn in a way. All those things that seemed important on land seemed so insignificant when we were cruising. Your values change. Or maybe they don't change so much as you rediscover who you are and what the really important things in life are.*

My partner and I found too that our move to a cruising lifestyle had a strong impact on our land life, and cruising caused us to alter the way we lived on land.

Twenty months before my study on the cruising lifestyle was formally completed, my partner suggested that we sell our house in the city and downsize to a house in the country. His reasons were compelling.

We were not employed exclusively in the city where we lived, and our private practices were portable; our property taxes had increased fourfold in the ten years since we purchased the house; and our house was very large and expensive to maintain. He then added the icing on the cake: he felt we would be healthier in the country, for we would be able to work less ow-ing to reduced expenses; we would have more time for cruising; and (this is the one that really got my attention) it was likely we could maintain a land base while we were cruising.

As sagacious as his arguments were, I found myself refuting each one. "I need to be close to the university to finish my study," I said. "We'll stay within two hours of the university," he said. "I need to have access to an airport so I can fly out to my clients," I said. "We'll stay within two hours of the airport," he replied.

I argued that country living could turn out to be more expensive than city living. We'd need to purchase a second vehicle—likely a four-wheel drive to handle snow and sleet. I asked my partner whether he had considered the ramifications of country living: septic fields and well water versus the accessible city systems. "You'll have to shovel snow!" I warned him (something he abhorred when we lived in the far north several years prior). "I'll buy a snowblower!" he retorted. "You hate the cold!" I reminded him. "I'll *love* winter in the country," he replied, with a grin on his face. And so it went for months.

I finally agreed to think about it, with the provision that we wouldn't move until I had completed my study. As you've probably figured out by now, I was resisting a move because it represented yet another major lifestyle change. I had grown attached to the perennial gardens I'd created around our house in the city, and I was fond of my neighbor directly across the street; she was the only person on the block that I'd come to know in the ten years we'd lived in that neighborhood. Goods and services were very accessible to us, too: we lived within walking distance to a fish market, an Italian meat market, a bakery, a European delicatessen, a florist, a travel agent, the dry cleaner, and so much more. I liked being able to walk our dog on the sidewalks, under the protective glare of streetlights in the wee hours of the morning and late at night. And I had come to embrace the cruising lifestyle that we were working toward. We were spending increasing amounts of time on the boat, and I was already walking a tightrope, gingerly balancing the demands of my career, my study, and my family. I didn't have time to move, even if I wanted to.

But a few months later, something remarkable occurred. We were driving home from Georgian Bay that summer. Each time we stopped for coffee, I picked up a complimentary issue of the local real-estate listings. As my partner drove along, I surveyed the listings and found myself saying how beautiful they sounded: an acre or two of land, groves of maple trees, a year-round trout stream, a panoramic view, and a house to boot! We read about a little piece of land with a spectacular view and decided to look at it.

We found the land after several hours of meandering through a stunning countryside that took us to the top of a mountain overlooking the Bay. The panoramic view was breathtaking, but the land had been sold. So we continued toward home.

That night I sent a fax to the agent we had contacted about the land. I described the kind of real estate we were looking for (not that I was looking!), and I listed all the features we wanted. My partner read my wish list and said with a sigh, "With a list like this, we'll never leave the city." But I believe when something is meant to be, the universe will conspire to make it happen. And so it was for us.

The following morning the agent called with a list of three homes that met our criteria. We drove north that same day, looked at the first one, fell head over heels in love with it, and placed an offer on it that night. Within three weeks, we had sold our home in the city and packed up and moved to the country. It really happened that quickly.

The day we moved in, four neighbors came by to welcome us to the area, and our friendships have since developed. We pick up each other's mail, let pets out when one of us plans to be away for the day, and watch each other's homes when a neighbor is away. When not on *Beedahbun* or *Red Witch*, we pursue our passions for cross-country skiing, cycling, and hiking. Wild-flowers take the place of time-demanding lawns, and we are tracking the bird species that frequent the feeder outside our kitchen window. Even our dog, once a timid tulip who cowered when our city neighbors changed the color of their garbage bags, has become a somewhat fearless tiger; she too seems to have come into her own from the changes we've made.

Over time, we've managed to establish a life on land and a life on the water—and they complement each other. In the country, we have been able to replicate the simplicity we found in cruising.

Cruising gives you the opportunity to take stock of your life. For most, it is the ultimate time-out from a rat race that has so many people feeling lost and frazzled. Cruising is a simpler, less encumbered lifestyle, and it offers you an opportunity for self-discovery and growth—an opportunity to explore your soul as you try to make sense of your place in this constantly changing world.

The cruising lifestyle is not forever, but it is a passage in your life that will forever have an impact on who you are and how you live. After reading this book, you now know that *Changing Course* is not simply a guide on trading your land life for a life on the water: it is about all that you stand to gain when you dare to make this lifestyle change.

My partner's dream of the cruising life has forever changed the course of our lives. You too can change your course and bring a sense of magic and renewal to your life. The choice is yours.

~~~

*APPENDIX*

# Demographics and Procedures

THE DEMOGRAPHIC DATA THAT FOLLOWS WAS compiled from a written questionnaire that participants completed before being interviewed and from their responses to interview questions. A sampling of exploratory questions is provided. These questions invariably generated lengthy and wide-ranging discussions from which many of the key themes in the study emerged.

## DEMOGRAPHIC INFORMATION ABOUT STUDY PARTICIPANTS

Age Distribution:
    < 35 years of age: 17%
    36–45 years of age: 44%
    46–55 years of age: 21%
    56–65 years of age: 10%
    > 65 years of age: 7%

Employment Status:
    Employed in professional career prior to making the change: 75%
    Unemployed or homemaker: 25%

Marital/Relationship Status and Family Circumstances:
    First marriage or common-law relationship: 16%
    Married prior to current partner: 42%

Married or living together < 5 years when partner expressed desire to make a change: 55%

Married > 20 years when partner expressed desire to make a change: 12%

With the same partner after cruising or when in last contact with this writer: 91%

Cruised with children: < 5%

Women at specific stages of making the change at the time of the interview:

Stage 1: Just talking about it: 3%

Stage 2: Committed to the concept: 10%

Stage 3: Boat purchased: 32%

Stage 4: Living aboard vessel: 18%

Stage 5: Cruising: 20%

Stage 6: Back on land: 18%

Women who returned to land and have since resumed cruising: 84%

Average length of time that passed from when the initiating partner first revealed his desire to go cruising until the couple actually began the process of making the change: 4.5 years

Women who:

initially resisted the change: 80%

initiated or embraced the change from the outset: 20%

eventually made the change: 95%

had "little or no" prior sailing experience: 78%

were "very" or "fairly" satisfied with land life before going cruising: 88%

derived an "enormous" or "large" amount of happiness and life satisfaction from choosing to cruise: 80%

retained a land base or other real estate: 70%

regretted having made the lifestyle change: 0%

# SAMPLE QUESTIONS FROM THE INTERVIEWS

Let's begin by talking about the change. Tell me about the lifestyle change initiated by your partner. How long had he talked about his desire to go cruising? How did his revelation change your life? What changed?

Looking back over the total experience, from when your partner presented you with the notion of going cruising/living on a boat, throughout the planning stages, and after the change had in fact occurred, what were the most difficult or challenging aspects for you?

Describe the extent of your sailing experience when your partner first proposed the cruising lifestyle. Have you done any overnight sailing? Any offshore voyaging? Of what duration?

How does your experience as a sailor compare to that of your partner?

To what extent has making the change altered your level of independence? Do you feel a greater sense of independence? A lesser sense? Unchanged? What factors have contributed to your greater (or lesser) sense of independence?

In your questionnaire you checked off feelings that described your initial reaction to your partner's expressed desire to make the change. Tell me more about where these feelings came from. For example, "anger" at whom or because of what? What other feelings do you recall experiencing at that time?

I'm interested in how your thoughts and feelings evolved or changed from when you first heard about the notion of living on a boat until the time when the process of making the change was underway. For example, was there a point at which your feelings subsided or intensified. Can you recall an event or series of events or circumstances that led to this?

How supportive has your partner been throughout the change process?

Would you describe your partner as your best friend?

I'm also interested in any actions you personally may have taken that correspond with the feelings you had at the time. Can you recall activities and/or actions that corresponded with your thoughts and feelings as they evolved? For example, did you go to the library or bookstore and purchase a book about sailing out of curiosity? How did you deal with any fears?

What effect, if any, did your feelings have on your relationship with your partner? For example, when you were feeling _____, what were you thinking/feeling about your partner? About your relationship?

Do you believe the cruising lifestyle has changed your relationship with your partner? Made it stronger? More vulnerable? More enriched? Been detrimental to it?

Did it ever occur to you that you did not have to support your partner's proposed change? Did you believe you had the option of not going cruising? What did you think would happen to your partner, to you, to your relationship, if you did not support the proposed change?

Oftentimes, the notion of change overwhelms us with a sense of loss. Can you recall thinking about what you stood to lose if the change occurred? Probe: proximity to family, friends; familiarity of neighborhood, community; security; career opportunities; material possessions; financial freedoms; etc.

Did you sell your home? Any regrets? How did you manage storage of precious items?

Initially, did you think about what you personally would gain by living on a boat/going cruising? At what point did you begin to think more about what you'd gain by the change and less about what you'd lose? Probe: what types of activities have you experienced while living aboard/cruising that have enriched your life?

Was there a point at which your partner's proposed change went from being "his plan" to "our plan"? Do you recall when this happened and what led to it? How did your "ownership" in the plan at this point change your perceptions of what your partner was proposing? Probe: to what extent were you involved in the selection of your vessel?

Is there a point on the continuum where you began to actively work with your partner toward making the change? What sorts of things do you recall doing?

This is a hard question, and I'll understand if you don't want to answer it. Sometimes when someone we're close to proposes something that we really are opposed to, we consciously or unconsciously "sabotage" their plans. I realize that "sabotage" is a strong word—perhaps the word "derail" is more appropriate. Let me give you an example. Do you recall at any point from the time your partner shared his desire to make a change until it became a reality, doing anything else along this line? What did you do?

In your questionnaire, you indicate that this much time,_____, elapsed from when you first heard about your partner's desire to make the change until it was implemented. During this time, how much did you and your partner talk about the overall implications of the change: A lot? Fairly often? For a few hours each day? Not at all?

In retrospect do you wish you and your partner had talked about the change: More often? Less often? Or did you talk about it enough?

What aspects of the cruising lifestyle/living on a boat do you wish you had talked about more?

While you were in the process of making the change, who in your life (besides your partner) was most supportive of the change (friends, family, colleagues, clergy, etc.)? Were any of these individuals instrumental in helping you feel more or less positive about the proposed change? Probe: what did they say or do?

A lot of women have looked at their partners when they proposed living on a boat and said "not on your life" or something similar, and that ended any further talk about the issue. What makes you different from them? How come you didn't react this way?

Overall, how has living on a boat/the cruising lifestyle changed you? Benefited you? Been detrimental to you? Affected other aspects of your life? Brought about more changes for you?

As a consequence of your partner's desire to make a lifestyle change, what sorts of activities and learnings—both formal and informal—did you undertake that, prior to the change, you had never imagined doing/exploring? Probe: interests, hobbies, specialized courses, training, formal education.

How much has this change contributed to your happiness, your satisfaction with life, and your well being? An enormous amount? A large amount? Somewhat? Not much at all? Done you more harm than good?

Is there anything else you would like to share with me that might benefit other women whose partners want them to live on a boat/go cruising?

ADDITIONAL QUESTIONS INCLUDED:

How long have you lived on your vessel/been cruising?

Did you live on your vessel for a period of time before you actually sailed off? For how long? How would you describe this period of the change process?

Do you take respites from the boat? How often? Where do you go?

Do you have any regrets about having made the change proposed by your partner?


Twenty years from now
you will be more
disappointed by the
things you didn't do
than by the ones
you did.
So throw off the bowlines.
Sail away from
the safe harbor.
Catch the trade winds
in your sails.
Explore. Dream. Discover.

# Bibliography

## GOOD BOOKS TO HAVE ON BOARD

Berkow, Robert, et al., ed., *The Merck Manual of Medical Information*, home edition. Whitehouse Station, New Jersey: Merck Research Laboratories, 1997.

Cameron, Julia. *The Artist's Way: A Spiritual Path to Higher Creativity*. Los Angeles: Jeremy P. Tarcher/Perigee, 1992.

Cornell, Jimmy. *World Cruising Routes*, 4th ed. Camden, Maine: International Marine, 1995.

Dear, Ian, and Kemp, Peter, eds. *An A–Z of Sailing Terms*. New York: Oxford University Press, 1992.

Graedon, Joe and Graedon, Teresa. *The People's Pharmacy, Completely New and Revised*. New York: St. Martin's Press, 1996.

Leonard, Beth A. *The Voyager's Handbook: The Essential Guide to Bluewater Cruising*. Camden, Maine: International Marine, 1998.

Royce, Patrick M. *Royce's Sailing Illustrated: The Best of All Sailing Worlds*. Newport Beach, California: Royce Publications, 1993.

Toss, Brion. *Knots*. New York: Hearst Marine Books, 1990.

Van Sant, Bruce. *The Gentleman's Guide to Passages South: Including Hispaniola and Puerto Rico: The Thornless Path to Windward*. Clearwater, Florida: B. Van Sant, 1989.

## SOURCES

Adams, John, John Hayes, and Barrie Hopson. *Transition: Understanding and Managing Personal Change.* London: Martin Robertson, 1976.

Anderson, Peggy, comp. *Great Quotes from Great Women.* Franklin Lakes, New Jersey: Career Press, 1997.

Bridges, William. *Transitions: Making Sense of Life's Changes.* Reading, Massachusetts: Addison-Wesley, 1980.

Cooper, Bill, and Cooper, Laurel. *Sell Up and Sail: Taking the Ulysses Option,* 3rd ed. Dobbs Ferry, New York: Sheridan House, 1998.

Cooper, Bill, and Cooper, Laurel. *Watersteps through France: To the Camargue by Canal.* Dobbs Ferry, New York: Sheridan House, 1996.

Cornell, Jimmy. *World Cruising Routes,* 4th ed. Camden, Maine: International Marine, 1995.

Frankel, Michael L., ed. *Gently with the Tides: The Best of Living Aboard.* Camden, Maine: International Marine, 1993.

Gray, John. *Men Are from Mars, Women Are from Venus: A Practical Guide for Improving Communication and Getting What You Want in Your Relationships.* New York: HarperCollins, 1992.

Hendrix, Harville. *Getting the Love that You Want: A Guide for Couples.* New York: Perennial Library, 1990.

Hill, Annie. *Voyaging on a Small Income.* St. Michaels, Maryland: Tiller, 1993.

Kübler-Ross, Elisabeth. *On Death and Dying.* New York: Scribner Classics, 1997. Originally published in 1969, this book is now available in several editions.

Leonard, Beth A. *The Voyager's Handbook: The Essential Guide to Bluewater Cruising.* Camden, Maine: International Marine, 1998.

Maggio, Rosalie, comp. *The Beacon Book of Quotations by Women.* Boston: Beacon Press, 1992.

Maslow, Abraham H. *Toward a Psychology of Being*, 3rd ed. New York: John Wiley & Sons, 1999.

Massey, Hart. *Travels with "Lionel": A Small Barge in France.* London: Gollancz, 1988.

Oatley, Keith. "Role Transitions and the Emotional Structure of Everyday Life." In *On the Move: The Psychology of Change and Transition,* ed. Shirley Fisher and Cary L. Cooper. New York: John Wiley & Sons, 1990.

Shard, Paul, and Shard, Sheryl. *Sail Away!: A Guide to Outfitting and Provisioning for Cruising.* Mississauga, Ontario: Pelagic Press, 1995.

Spencer, Sabina A., and John D. Adams. *Life Changes: Growing through Personal Transitions.* San Luis Obispo, California: Impact, 1990.

Tough, Allen M. *Intentional Changes: A Fresh Approach to Helping People Change.* Chicago: Follett, 1982.

Viorst, Judith. *Necessary Losses: The Loves, Illusions, Dependencies and Impossible Expectations that All of Us Have to Give Up in Order to Grow.* New York: Simon & Schuster, 1986.

# About the Author

DEBRA ANN CANTRELL, HER HUSBAND, JIM, and first mate, Sydney, divide their time between a 36-foot Nauticat, *Beedahbun,* in the south, a 33-foot Chris-Craft, *Red Witch,* in the north, and a land base in Collingwood, Ontario, Canada.

Debra and her family began experiencing life on a boat in summer 1991 and continue to spend the summer months cruising Georgian Bay on the *Red Witch*. The lure of warmer seas and voyaging under sail beckoned in spring 1994. Since then, the Cantrells have continuously increased the amount of time they cruise and currently spend approximately six months each year living afloat.

Much of Debra's professional life has been devoted to the helping professions, in particular, to helping Canadian Native Indians become self-reliant and self-governing. Her specialty is facilitating workshops and seminars for helping professionals who are seeking balance and striving for wellness at work and play. In recent years, she has focused on the phenomenon of change. She delivers workshops for individuals and couples who are contemplating major lifestyle changes.

Debra finds her cruising and land-based lifestyles to be mutually enhancing, and she cannot imagine one without the other.